The vision of Spirit of Martyrdom for reaching the lost motivates us all. God has given this organization a special heart for the living martyrs worldwide, and a desire to raise people in His Word.

That desire shows clearly in this orality training and Spirit of Martyrdom lovingly shares this with others. How can we equip and empower people to share the Lord's truth with the lost? This workbook helps answer this question by giving everyone, regardless of literacy skills, the opportunity to learn an oral-based Scripture sharing method. Enjoy the process, dig deep in the Word and share with the world.

Andrea
Executive Director, The God's Story Project
Senior Instructor, Simply The Story

In making disciples, Jesus was quoted five times telling His disciples to "go and proclaim." Look at how Jesus applied His own exhortation. Over 40 times in the Gospels, Jesus goes out and talks to people, and in Matthew 13 we are told He never engaged a crowd without telling them a parable. These are just a few reasons to give serious attention to what Spirit of Martyrdom is doing to equip and encourage Christians anywhere in the world through the Witness Development Evangelism Workbook, especially those who are under duress. This manual represents Spirit of Martyrdom's commitment to get people into the Word and the Word into people, and then the Word out through people. I am so thankful to God to have a part in Spirit of Martyrdom's global effectiveness for the glory of God.

Dr. Jim Thurber

Over the course of 10 years, Youth 4 the Kingdom and Spirit of Martyrdom ministries have been working together in the mission field and have formed a close relationship. While on the mission field in 3rd world countries, we have found that the Witness Development Evangelism method is one of the most practical and effective foundational tool for teaching at all levels. The Witness Development Evangelism Workbook is designed to reach the deep spiritual Biblical truths of the scripture and at the same time, it is easy for a new believer to learn. We use this manual to teach discipleship and evangelism for all age groups. At Y4K, we strongly endorse and recommend this workbook. It is an effective and simple method to use and will be a blessing for you.

Daniel Chelmagan
President, Youth 4 The Kingdom

Spirit of Martyrdom's involvement in church planting and discipleship multiplication as a global mission has led us to discover a unique tool in ministering and evangelizing to others. The Witness Development Evangelism Workbook carries the transforming tools on how to effectively witness and disciple both schooled and unschooled people in any cultural context.

We have adopted the Witness Development Evangelism training in our Church Planting Schools and Lighthouse Sewing Schools. Every 6 months, 400-500 church planters graduate empowered with Witness Development Evangelism resources and training.

More than 8,000 house churches across the country of India have experienced the Witness Development Evangelism method. The church planters have expressed that using this method has been a great resource in witnessing and discipleship. We have experienced ordinary and even unschooled people who are effective witnesses of Jesus Christ as they share through Bible stories. The church planting and discipleship is multiplying across our country.

May the Lord Almighty use the Witness Development Evangelism Workbook in all the unreached and diverse cultures. Let there be rapid discipleship multiplication and expansion of God's kingdom around the world.

Pastor Singh
President of Church Planting Movement
SOM INDIA

WITNESS
DEVELOPMENT
EVANGELISM WORKBOOK

Check out "Witness Development Evangelism Training Description" by Spirit of Martyrdom:

WITNESS DEVELOPMENT
EVANGELISM WORKBOOK

Jesus-Style Conversational Evangelism

Instructor's Guide

David and Cindy Witt
Ron Kaufmann

ANEKO
PRESS

Visit the SOM website: www.spiritofmartyrdom.com

Witness Development Evangelism Workbook

David Witt, Cindy Witt, Ron Kaufmann

Cover Design: Amber Burger

Cover Photography: www.BillionPhotos.com/Shutterstock

Icon Images: from Freepik via FlatIcon.com

Editor: Michelle Rayburn

Printed in the United States of America

Aneko Press – *Our Readers Matter*™

www.anekopress.com

Aneko Press, Life Sentence Publishing, and our logos are trademarks of Life Sentence Publishing, Inc.
203 E. Birch Street
P.O. Box 652
Abbotsford, WI 54405

RELIGION / Christian Ministry / Evangelism

Paperback ISBN: 978-1-62245-287-3

Ebook ISBN: 978-1-62245-288-0

10 9 8 7 6 5 4 3 2 1

Available where books are sold.

Share this book on Facebook:

Contents

Acknowledgments and Introduction

by David Witt

Spirit of Martyrdom (SOM) exists for the glory of God by serving His church, the *living martyrs*, those who are witnessing their faith in Jesus Christ at great risk and sacrifice. Our mission statement includes "equipping Christians to serve as witnesses around the world." Whether it is a small group or a large group, we want to embolden the witness of the church. SOM wishes to share the best tools that we see God using around the world.

God is directing His global church back to His Word. We are observing the church explode in areas of the world as native Christians and missionaries share the Word of God with stories and inductive questions. (For more stories, please go to our website: www.SpiritofMartyrdom.com.) Universally, we have found that most everyone loves a good story and conversational questions. What is most important is that it is biblical. Throughout history, stories were used to teach important principles and nuggets of wisdom. Jesus used parables (stories) to communicate His message to the people. The Witness Development

Evangelism process is based upon these two premises: biblical teaching and biblical storytelling.

The SOM *Witness Development Evangelism Workbook* teaches a process for evangelism and outreach. This process came out of our growth in the discipleship method of the Oral Inductive Bible Study. We believe that the Oral Inductive Bible Study is one of the best discipleship tools for the Body of Christ today. The *Witness Development Evangelism Workbook* takes the principles of Oral Inductive Bible Study and provides an easy-to-use format to share with strangers, non-Christians and Christians alike, whether you have five minutes or fifty minutes to spend with someone. The teaching is also made to encourage reproduction and multiplication of sharing God's Word.

There are many individuals God used for the inspiration of this material. I would like to thank the SOM staff for their support and encouragement. Dorothy Miller, founder of *The God Story Project* (an 80-minute DVD narrative of Scriptures from Genesis to Revelation) and "Simply the Story" (a teaching method of Oral Inductive Bible Study) was an inspiration and a delight to work with. While we were compiling this *Witness Development Evangelism Workbook*, Dorothy passed into glory and is in the presence of her Lord and Savior. We will all miss her and will continue to be inspired by her legacy of hiding God's Word in our hearts. (You can go to www.SimplytheStory. org for more information.) Another person who I would like to acknowledge is Andrea, who is current director with Simply the Story (STS) and *The God Story Project*. Andrea has a passion for the Word of God and for people around the world. I believe it is a rare day that she does not witness a God story to someone along her path. Her teaching and friendship have been a tremendous blessing.

Dr. Jim Thurber has also made a remarkable impact for this *Witness Development Evangelism Workbook*. I am honored to call Jim a friend and he is an extraordinary evangelist. Jim is one of the most effective trainers I have worked with. He is a church planter and developed the Hi-Definition Discipleship Evangelism method using tools from the STS method. He is passionate about God's glory and how His glory is central to sharing the Gospel. (To contact Dr. Jim Thurber for speaking or training, please email: k9kq@me.com.)

The Holy Spirit also used the SOM domestic Muslim outreach team of Daniel Ted, Diane Duran, Carol Smith and Matthew Redondo in the development of this workbook. After Jim Thurber taught the SOM staff his Hyper-Discipler method, we were energized and encouraged with a very effective process. Daniel, Diane, Carol and Matthew agreed that we needed to develop four chronological Bible stories that work with all people, including Muslims. The stories they asked to develop were: "The Disobedience of Adam and Eve" (Genesis 3), "Abram and the Birth of Ishmael" (Genesis 16), "Abraham and Isaac" (Genesis 22) and "The Three Crosses" (Luke 23).

When sharing with Muslims, we have found the story of Abraham and Ishmael clearly demonstrates the heart of God to Muslims. It is a story that God has used in all of our lives to increase our love and hope for what God wants to do in the Muslim world and it is a great picture of God's redemptive plan to save people out of the kingdom of man into the kingdom of God.

SOM has now developed three 14-hour workshops to serve the global church: the Witness Development Evangelism Workshop, the Witness Development Discipleship Workshop and the Witness Development Muslim Outreach Workshop.

Our hope is that churches will desire to be equipped with all three workshops. The WD Evangelism Workshop and the WD Discipleship Workshop have been developed and refined with the specific help of SOM staff and Bible trainer Ron Kaufmann. The WD Muslim Outreach Workshop has come from much of the teaching and leadership of SOM Vice-President of Muslim Outreach, Daniel D. Ted, and his leadership team.

Last, but certainly not least, I want to thank my beautiful bride, Cindy, who is my deepest friend and partner in ministry. Ultimately, this is a work of God's grace and many members of the Body of Christ who support the work of Spirit of Martyrdom ministries around the world.

Regarding Reproduction of the Witness Development Evangelism Workbook

Since Spirit of Martyrdom ministries exists for the glory of God by serving the church, we believe that God governs over the ministry and our personal lives. Therefore, He receives all glory and rights to this manual. We hope that this process will strengthen the witness of Christ and will be reproduced throughout the world. The *Witness Development Evangelism Workbook* and workshops are designed to give participants a global and local kingdom vision.

One term we use in referring to the discipleship of Christians is that each of us will have a *"glocal"* (global and local) worldview. In this spirit, we encourage you to use and share this material with others. We have only two requests: that you notify us of your intent through the contact form on our website, and that you include reference to our website (www.SpiritofMartyrdom.com) when reproducing this material. This helps us to connect with participants for further teaching and information as needed.

PART I

The Witness Development Evangelism Method

The Witness Development Evangelism method is best learned in a workshop. It uses oral, kinetic, and visual learning styles. The *Witness Development Evangelism Workbook* is designed for many leaders to participate up front and in small groups. We found this format of co-leading to be effective.

This workbook is written to help with preparation and review of the evangelism process. We believe there is great value in reading through this material and gleaning valuable concepts. We hope you will be encouraged and equipped by reading this workbook. Please keep in mind that we believe reading this is not equal to experiencing a weekend workshop where you can practice the illustrations in partnership with others. After reading this manual, please consider hosting a workshop in your area or attending a workshop. You will find more information at: www.SpiritofMartyrdom.com.

Preparation and Sponsoring a Workshop

Preparation is key to a productive workshop. The first step is securing a SOM Lead Instructor and setting a weekend date by contacting us at: contact@SpiritofMartyrdom.com. A minimum of two months is needed to organize a workshop successfully. A

Lead Instructor is someone who SOM has identified as a leader who is competent in every aspect of the Witness Development Evangelism process and the ministry of Spirit of Martyrdom. Our hope is to see many Christians trained who then serve as instructors who train others.

Responsibilities of the host church or organization

Manage registration

- Registration is necessary for participants of the workshop. Forms are available from our office at contact@SpiritofMartyrdom.com.

- Registration creates a commitment from participants, as there are many people investing in them. A concrete number of participants will help to plan the weekend better.

- A registration fee will help to offset the costs of the hosting church/group for the snacks, meals, and any other overhead. This also may provide assistance for someone who cannot afford to attend, if the organization would like to sponsor him or her. Money should never be a reason for someone not to attend.

- Registration allows SOM and the church to have contact information of participants for follow up and discipleship.

Permit the SOM Lead Instructor to give a Sunday message

- The host church, organization, or small group will allow the SOM Lead Instructor to encourage the Body of Christ with a message for the morning worship services.

- The instructor will illustrate biblical principles with testimonies of persecuted believers overcoming and will emphasize our call to be courageous witnesses of Jesus Christ.

- An optional Sunday evening celebration service is suggested for your congregation to come hear testimonies from workshop participants. This will also give the workshop participants an immediate opportunity to practice their newfound skills.

Take a love offering

- Spirit of Martyrdom ministries does not charge a fee for speaking, teaching, or presenting. All that we ask is that a love offering be taken to help offset the travel expenses and for the overall work of Spirit of Martyrdom.

Promote the workshop

- The host church commits to promote the training with its local congregation and community.

Accommodate needs of participants

- We ask the host church to provide snacks and drinks throughout the training, optionally provide a Friday dinner, provide Saturday lunch, and optionally provide a Sunday dinner in connection with a celebration service.

- Additionally, the host church should help with transportation and lodging when available.

Select five to eight Assistant Instructors.

- We need a high level of commitment from the church, organization or group interested in being trained. SOM asks for five to eight leaders from your church or organization who will serve as Assistant Instructors with the training in presenting assigned materials in up-front presentations.

- This *Witness Development Evangelism Workbook* will be distributed ahead of time to the Assistant Instructors. The Lead Instructor will assign sections to Assistant Instructors to study in order to present illustrations during the workshop.

- There are 46 sections or illustrations in the Witness Development Evangelism Workshop. The Lead Instructor will take the most comprehensive and difficult sections.

- In our 14-hour weekend training, it is our ultimate goal to effectively hand off the skills and tools for

the participants to share with others. As the local
Assistant Instructors invest in learning the material, it is natural that they will be able to reproduce
the training within their church and spheres of
influence to multiply the tools in sharing Christ
with others.

Coaching for Assistant Instructors

Thank you for volunteering to assist as an instructor for
the Witness Development Evangelism Workshop. Assistant
Instructors often report they grow more than other participants
because of their leadership role in this workshop. We hope you
will be blessed as you serve. SOM's goal is to help you enjoy the
process and to feel successful in learning the tools. The SOM
Lead Instructor is your personal coach to give you competence
in your assignment. In the end, it is our hope that you will be so
energized by the Witness Development Evangelism process that
you will want to teach others and participate in more Witness
Development Evangelism Workshops.

The paradigm of the Witness Development Evangelism Workshop
is that we present all the material without notes or scripts. We
want all the information stored in the hearts of the presenters
first so that the Bible stories will be presented conversationally
with passion, confidence and long-term retention. Presenting
this information orally with many leaders constantly changing up front produces a dynamic atmosphere. We have found
that this method of oral teaching creates energy, attentiveness,
a quicker transfer of information, higher retention of information and greater group participation. It is truly hiding God's
Word in your "heart pocket."

Many people report how surprised they are by how fast time flies and how they can retain God's Word and enjoy mining for the treasures in the Scriptures by applying this method of learning Scripture. The tools in this method will equip you to share with your neighbor or in a foreign country. It can help people who are illiterate learn God's living and breathing Word and hide it in their hearts.

The first thing you should do is complete the questionnaire the Lead Instructor will email to you. (The questionnaire is in the Appendix of this *Witness Development Evangelism Workbook*.) The questionnaire will help the Lead Instructor discern the best sections to assign to you to learn and present.

Once you have received your assignments from the Lead Instructor, you will begin to learn your sections. How you learn the sections is part of the process of growth in this workshop. At first, you may have to trust us by faith that this process works. This process is a proven method and it does work. **We are not asking you to memorize the sections.** We want you to learn the material and understand each concept so that you can use your own conversational language and feel natural about telling it. Here is how we would like you to learn each assigned section of the *Witness Development Evangelism Workbook*:

1. Read each assigned section slowly and aloud. Read the **whole section** before stopping.

2. Close your eyes and repeat back as much as you remember. Do not peek at the text and cheat.

3. Again, read the **whole section aloud**.

4. Close your eyes. Repeat as much as you remember, and this time try to picture the actions and concepts as you speak it aloud. With your eyes closed, add gestures and hand movements, as this helps greatly by using kinetic memory.

5. Repeat this method until you feel confident about the material.

Some encouragement to help you prepare

- Go ahead and memorize the first sentence so you can get started. Getting started is sometimes the hardest part.

- Some people have reported that recording themselves and listening to the section helps them learn the section better.

- Ask a friend to read the section to you aloud.

- Some people have reported they learn the section better by standing and moving while they listen and repeat back the section.

- Other people have found making a story board of their section helpful. A story board is drawing a picture for each concept or illustration within your section. Search "story boarding" on www.YouTube. com for more help.

- Be encouraged! We have found that most people have over 70% accuracy in using this method after just ten minutes of following this plan. Most people will find 90% to 100% accuracy within twenty minutes.

- Remember, communicating the concepts is what is most important. Therefore, using various conversational words and even changing the order of the presentation in each written section is fine, as long as the meaning is not changed.

- We are all products of God's grace. The Witness Development Evangelism Workshop leaders are full of grace. We want every Assistant Instructor to have fun in their participation and laugh when needed to relieve any pressure to perform. The Witness Development Evangelism Workshop is about presenting the truth. Jesus came with grace and truth. Therefore, we need to present the truth with grace.

- SOM leaders and the Witness Development Evangelism process practice co-leadership. With a plurality of leadership, leaders can serve each other by contributing their knowledge and helping one another in competence by presenting the information as a team. In the workshop, we give all the information without reading or using notes up front. Lead Instructors co-lead each other to help refresh and remember sections. This takes the pressure off any one person to have all the knowledge and removes unrealistic perfectionism. For instance, an instructor may be presenting a section and completely forget where they are. A Lead

Instructor will cue them for what is to be shared next, or if encouraged by the presenter, will get up and take over and teach the rest of the section in a spirit of joy and cooperation. We teach co-leading at the beginning of the workshop so that participants understand what we are doing and expect teamwork in our instruction.

- The Lead Instructor will contact you and schedule an appointment with you via phone or Skype. The appointment will be held within 10 days of the workshop. The Lead Instructor will help you practice your sections and coach you in confidence and presentation.

PART II

Witness Development Evangelism

Friday Night Workshop

Introduction to the Workshop

Welcome everyone to Spirit of Martyrdom's Witness Development Workshop. Introduce yourself and who you are. Thank the partner host ministry for making this possible. Make sure everyone has a SOM newsletter and hold up one for everyone to see. If anyone does not have a newsletter, then get him or her one. Tell them to look on the back to read the SOM mission purpose. Explain to the group that during this next 14 hours, you hope to accomplish two points of the Spirit of Martyrdom mission purpose:

- *Equipping* Christians to serve as witnesses around the world

- *Presenting* Muslims with the witness of Jesus Christ

Let the group know the rest of the SOM mission purpose points are listed on the back of the newsletter.

The following is a template for Lead Instructors. This is a guide for you to follow as you prepare for the workshop. Again, we don't want you to memorize this or to read from the workbook as you lead, but learn the material and put it into your own words.

Lead Instructor Template

Our hope is to make the most of every moment of our workshop. This is an interactive workshop with hands-on training and immediate implementation. As we have devoted ourselves to you by handing off these amazing tools, we ask that you will devote yourselves to this time by setting aside all outside distractions and to focus on what God wants to do with you.

Please take out your cell phones and hold them up. Are they on silent mode? [Pause for response.] Great, if they do ring during our teaching sessions, we are happy to confiscate them and you may retrieve them after the workshop via eBay. We all understand that life happens and the unexpected can take place during this workshop. If there truly is an emergency, then we ask that you take your call outside so that it will not be distracting to others.

Our host has provided food and drinks. We will try to have a break at least every two hours. Please make the best effort to be punctual, present and attentive as sessions begin. The 14 hours for this training will be divided into 3 1/2 hours tonight (Friday), 7 hours tomorrow (Saturday), and 3 1/2 hours on (Sunday).

Unique Teaching Style

Orality works. How many of you are ready to learn and have brought a pen and paper for notes? [Pause for response.]

Impressive! Now go ahead and put them away. You will **not** be using them for this workshop. Our Witness Development Evangelism Workshop is different in that we present all the material in an oral learning fashion.

First, we are teaching in a way to develop your mental muscles to be able to recall the information without notes. If you use notes while evangelizing, then the information may be presented in a manner lacking confidence, thus possibly hindering the validity of the message to the listener.

Second, keep in mind that life-changing ideas and events are easily recalled without notes. Also, we know and trust that we have divine help to recall this information. In John 14, we are promised that the Holy Spirit will bring all these things into remembrance. For those who love to take notes, we will give the *Witness Development Evangelism Workbook* at the end.

Other Distinctives About Our Witness Development

The oral method is very effective in the transferring of information to non-literates, literates, and preferred oral learners alike. It helps to train and reach a broader range of people for Jesus.

We practice co-leading. Witness Development Evangelism is most effective as many leaders contribute their skills. Every leader is unique in his or her gift set and talents. Every leader is a learner and we all are refining our witnessing skills in this process. We have different levels of leaders, as each person is increasing in their proficiency and understanding of the Witness Development Evangelism process. We want to develop leadership in you and give you opportunities to practice teaching others.

For this reason, Witness Development Evangelism emphasizes multiplication. Not only do we want you to improve and find success in sharing the gospel, we also want to help you teach others to boldly and effectively share the gospel. From the biblical perspective, we call this discipleship.

It may feel chaotic at times, but try to remember there is a method to our madness. Participation can be messy, but this is the best way to develop competency in leaders. Please try new things, volunteer and have fun.

Personal Stories

During this weekend, we hope you will get to know one another better. How many of you like nametags? [Pause for response.] Great, so do I. Please keep them on throughout the weekend and we will have lots of interaction to know each other better. Let's take a moment to get to know the person next to you. Turn to one or two people and each of you concisely share how you came to be at this workshop. You have three minutes to do this.

***

How many people just enjoyed sharing and hearing the reason for people coming? [Pause for response.] You all just shared a story. In America, how do we greet most people? [Wait for answer.] Yes, "How are you?" Most people give a very short response of "good" or "fine," but we invite them to tell more when interacting. The only thing people love more than listening to a story is telling their own stories. Everyone has some sort of story to tell and we connect emotionally with people through similar experiences in stories.

Listening and Responding

The second great commandment of God is what? [Pause for response.] Love our neighbor as our self. Everyone enjoys feeling that they have been heard. How many of you agree that you feel good when someone listens well to what you have to say? Raise your hands. What are some of the ways you can know if someone is listening well? [Pause for response.]

Some may share, "They look me in the eye," or "They listen to me with gestures (attentive body language)." Others may say, "Words of affirmation (they mirror my words by repeating them)."

Would you conclude that people who listen respond well? [Pause for response.] The Witness Development Evangelism Workshop is all about sharing our faith in Christ with others. Therefore, what should our first rule be when sharing our faith? [Pause for response.] (Answer: We must be active listeners and responders.)

To excel in this area, we need to learn to ask great questions. Most people love to talk with people who ask good questions. The second rule of Witness Development Evangelism is to ask questions. I want you to think of someone you know who asks good questions. What type of questions do they ask? How do they make you feel when you talk to them? What can you learn from their example? Take a minute and concisely share this with the person next to you.

***

Who can share with us some of the things you discovered about good questions? [Let the group share.]

God's Example of Using Questions

Who remembers the first recorded conversation with God in the Bible? In Genesis 3, we are told how God approached Adam after he disobeyed God by eating of the Tree of Knowledge of Good and Evil. God said to Adam, "Where are you?" God used a question. In what other ways could God have approached Adam in his disobedience? [Pause for response.] When we witness to others, are we confronting others with their disobedience? [Pause for response.]

What does "gospel" mean? [Pause for response.] Good news about what? [Pause for response.] Yes, God took our sins upon Himself so that now we are reconciled with Him.

We observe that God knew where Adam was and what he had done. Ultimately, God knew how Adam would answer. Yet, God still used a question and then let him answer.

If God uses the conversational approach of using a question to confront disobedience, what is the best way for us to confront others in their disobedience against God? Use questions!

God's Example of Listening and Responding

Let's talk about God's example of listening and responding.

Is prayer important to God? [Pause for response.]

How do we know this? Can you think of some examples or verses in the Scriptures? [Pause for response.]

Does God know what we are going to say before we say it? [Pause for response.]

Does God know what we need before we ask? [Pause for response.]

Yet, God commands us to pray and tells us that we are to pray unceasingly and we are to be a house of prayer. What do we learn about God? [Pause for response] (Answer: God loves to hear from and listens to His children!)

We see a biblical pattern of God using questions through His prophets and His Word. God loves hearing our answers. For Witness Development Evangelism, we use questions so that we can listen and respond.

Stories Communicate Truth

We are told that God, through the Holy Spirit, inspired His prophets to write the books of the Bible. God could have arranged the Bible in any order. Do we find any books of the Bible called "Justice of God" or a book called, "Love?" [Pause for response.] Or how about a book called "Faithfulness?" [Pause for response.]

God did not choose to arrange the Bible according to topics. What did God mostly use? [Pause for response.] [Hold up the Bible.] That's right, stories. God wove His character and attributes of justice, love, faithfulness, and more all together into the stories of the Bible. Certainly, since God designed us, He knows the best way that we learn. If God used stories in communicating His truth to us, then what might we use in communicating His truth to others? [Pause for response.] Yes, we use stories.

World Literacy

I want to share some interesting results from studies of American literacy.[1] [Get four volunteers to stand up front. Pick the most knowledgeable and confident person to represent the non-literate people of the world. Give them a book, pen and reading glasses, if available.] These four people represent the literacy rates of the United States. Non-literate, functionally non-literate, preferred oral and literate.

[Put your hand over the first person representing the non-literate.] Who do you think this person represents? [Help them get the answer quickly.] Why is it hard to guess that this person is non-literate? [If no one comments on the fact that the person has a pen and a Bible, prompt them a little.] "Hmm. Do you see something unusual about this person who never learned to read?" [Give attendees a chance to notice the book and/or the pen. If no one notices the items, give more of a hint.] "What is in his pocket?" or "What is in his hand?" [Eventually, attendees will notice.]

Sadly in some cultures literacy is used to measure people and those who have not had an opportunity to learn to read are not respected. To fit in, people will pretend to be literate by carrying a pen in their pocket or carrying a newspaper or a book.

In a developed country such as the USA, a country that tries to provide education for everyone, what percentage of people do you think cannot read? [Give a chance for guesses.] Actually, in the USA, 14% of the people are non-literate.

---

1   From Literacy and Oral Communication chapter in *Simply the Story Instructor's Manual*, pg.87)

This next person [say name] represents the functionally non-literate people. Functionally non-literate can read words, but struggle with sentences and have never read a book. What do you think is the percentage that this group represents? [Pause for answer.] Functionally non-literates represent 29% of the USA population.

Now this is interesting. [Take one hand and gently move the first two people sideways a few steps.] This means that how many in the USA cannot learn from reading? Can anyone add those percentages of the first two groups? [Give time for response of 43%.] Wow! 43%. That is nearly half of the people in the USA that can't really learn from written information.

Well, [say name] represents the preferred oral communicators group. This becomes really interesting. 44% of the people in the USA are preferred oral learners. They can read, but they prefer oral communication. If you give them the choice between reading the book or seeing the movie, this group will prefer to see the movie. They may read only one book a year and that book is usually required because of their profession. Isn't it amazing how many educated people, even highly educated, prefer oral communication?

Now we have what percent of people in the USA who cannot, or prefer not to, learn from reading? [Give time to respond.] 87%. Amazing!

That leaves our last group who are ....? [Give time to respond.] Highly literate. For those of you who are math experts, what percent are they? [Give time to respond.] 13% are highly literate.

Some say oral communication is mind *and* heart connection.

If the percentage of people in the USA who cannot, or do not prefer to learn from reading is this high, what must it be in other countries? Actually, in Canada and developed Europe, the statistics are the same as in the USA. Canadian researchers did the test twice because they didn't believe the results.

In some countries, the literacy rate, those who can read and understand what they have read, is as low as two or three percent. In order to not appear behind in education, some countries lower the standard of literacy to, "If you can sign your name, you are literate." The Encyclopedia Britannica will not even publish literacy rates for many emerging nations. This is because they know that the information submitted to them is way too high, misrepresented to make the country's citizens appear more literate than they really are.

By the way, of the four categories of learners [gesture to the four in line] we showed regarding literacy in the USA, which people do you think are most likely to design and write the Christian curriculum for the United States to use and material for mission outreach? [Gesture to each person individually and wait for people to respond, starting with the non-literate and move across to the highly literate.] The non-literate? The functionally non-literate? The preferred oral communicators? [When you come to the preferred oral communicator you may say, "Yes, they might, if you paid them enough!"] It is the last group.

The highly literate people are most likely to write the curriculum, and we are thankful for all of the good commentaries and theological information produced over the centuries by the highly literate communicators. Largely, they are the diligent ones who have translated Scripture so people of varied languages can hear from God in their own languages. We thank God for the ways they have applied their education. These literate communicators write ideas and present them with precise vocabulary, which can, and has, greatly benefited all these other kinds of learners. [Sweep arm across to indicate people representing the other three categories.]

If we think about it, since the invention of the printing press, what has been the predominate style used by the highly literate to wrap Scripture for use in evangelism, discipleship and missions? Oral or literate? [Wait for response.] Based on what we now see regarding the reality of who can read and who prefers to read, what might that show us about the amount of people in the world who can understand the dominant style of Christian communication? Isn't it time now to add some options to the way we communicate God's Word?

Praise God, we now are more aware that a large percentage of the world cannot or does not prefer to learn through literate methods. In response to that knowledge, we need to make sure more programs and material will be produced for evangelism and discipleship that are designed to be understood by those oral learners. They too need to know Jesus and need to be nurtured to grow in knowledge and grace.

Jesus' Model

Based on the 87% who cannot, or prefer not, to learn from literate methods, I wonder what God has done to communicate with us? How did Jesus communicate? [Pause for answer. If people have some Bible knowledge, they may respond with "parables" and "stories." If they do not know this, you can tell attendees of Jesus' use of stories and parables.] Ah maybe He didn't graduate from Torah school? After all, He was just a carpenter. [Pause] No? Oh, I know. He had to speak in stories for the uneducated. But wait. How did Jesus speak to the Pharisees, Scribes and Sadducees? Did He ever use stories? Yes, He did and they understood the message. Some even believed.

Could Jesus have given the most stunning lectures, using the most impressive vocabulary in existence? Yes, He could have. But Jesus chose to use words that the common working people of his day could understand, not the words that would only be understood by the most educated people in Jesus' day.

Note also the Bible format. [Reach over and pick up Bible.] This Bible is 75% stories, 15% poetry and 10% expositional. What do we predominantly use in Christian teaching? Maybe it is time to rethink.

We saw that Jesus often spoke in parables and told stories. But Jesus very often used another tool of communication. Repeatedly, Jesus gave His disciples and others a chance to think and to answer questions that would utilize a godly perspective. Out of the nearly 200 times Jesus was asked a question, Jesus responded with a direct answer only a few times. All the other times, Jesus responded by asking a question, telling a story or parable, or he was simply silent. Usually, after telling a story, Jesus asked a question and invited discussion. For three years, Jesus continued to train His disciples by encouraging them to listen to and recall His Word, to think and believe and to apply the wisdom. Jesus led by example in the use of stories and questions as a way to witness and disciple.

PART III

Witness Development Evangelism

Friday Night Workshop

Learn the First Story – The Disobedience of Adam and Eve (Genesis 3)

I n this training, we don't toss you ideas without applying them, so after all this talk about the use of stories, are you ready to learn your first story? I am going to teach you an effective way to learn a story from the Bible. This is the part where we need you to try new things. As I tell the story, I want you to picture the story in your mind as if you are watching a movie.

These are real stories from the Bible that have been inspired by the Holy Spirit. We understand that God's word cannot be understood unless the Spirit of God reveals it to us. So, before we learn any story or read God's Word, who might we want to ask for help in learning and understanding the story? Let's pray for the Holy Spirit to help us learn the story.

The Disobedience of Adam and Eve

As I tell the story, notice I insert names in place of pronouns. This slight paraphrasing helps the listener recall the story better.

[Tell story with animation]

> *So when the woman saw that the fruit was good*
> *for food, and that it was a delight to the eyes, and*
> *that the fruit was to be desired to make one wise,*
> *Eve took the fruit and ate, and she also gave some*
> *to her husband who was with her, and Adam ate.*
> *Then the eyes of both were opened, and they knew*
> *that they were naked. And Adam and Eve sewed fig*
> *leaves together and made themselves clothes. And*
> *Adam and Eve heard the sound of the LORD God*
> *walking in the garden in the cool of the day, and the*
> *man and his wife hid themselves from the presence*
> *of the LORD God among the trees of the garden. But*
> *the LORD God called to the man and said to him,*
> *"Where are you?" And Adam said, "I heard your*
> *voice in the garden, and I was afraid, because I was*
> *naked, and I hid myself."*

(Genesis 3:6-10 paraphrased from ESV)

Now, turn to the person next to you and have one of you repeat back as much as you remember. Start with, "So when the woman saw the fruit was good for food…" I promise all of you will score 100% because the assignment is *just* to repeat as much as *you* remember. [Give people time to complete the story.]

***

I am going to repeat the story again. This time I want to encourage you to close your eyes and picture the story happening. I suggest you use your hands and body to illustrate the story as I tell it; this will help to recall the story more accurately. [Tell the story again.]

Now, is there anyone who is willing to volunteer and stand up and tell as much of the story as they remember? Find a volunteer. [If no one volunteers, then have the participants turn to the same person as last time and the other person takes a turn telling the story.]

***

I am going to tell the story one more time. Remember, close your eyes, see the pictures, and use your hands. For those of you who are comfortable, I want you to stand up and try to enact the story with your eyes closed as I tell the story. We have found this helps to recall the story better. I remind you that we are all trying new things. If you're worried about looking funny, the only way that can happen is if you are the only one *not* doing the actions. Do not be tempted to be a "bump on a log" with no actions. Even small gestures are better than none and it will help you remember the story. [Tell the story.]

Now I need someone to stand up and volunteer to tell the story back as much as they remember. [Affirm the person enthusiastically.]

Accuracy, Actions and Expressions

Would you rather read a joke or hear it told? [Pause for people to respond.] There is something about how words delivered with expression can bring extra life to them. Would you rather have someone tell a story from God's Word in a monotone voice with little expression, or share a story from God's Word with actions and expressions that help us to feel the emotion of what is being communicated? [Pause for answer.] What do we like more? A story alive with expression or a story read with little expression? [Pause for answer.] We like lively stories.

We are presenting God's Word. We are told the great commandment is to love God and the second is to love others; therefore, if *we* prefer to hear God's Word this way, how should we communicate God's Word with others?

The Bible is God's Word, so is accuracy important? [Pause for answer.] Extremely important. In fact, God's Word warns that anyone who changes it by adding anything or subtracting anything will be cursed by God.

In the stories of Scripture, do they sometimes include the emotions felt? [Pause for answer.] Can anyone name a story in the Bible that includes the description of emotion? [Let them answer. After a bit, if they need help suggest a few.] How about the Pearl of Great Price parable? Does anyone remember the emotion felt by the merchant when he finds the pearl in the field? [Pause for answer.] (Joy.)

What emotion is usually mentioned at the appearance of an angel in the Bible? [Pause for answer.] (Fear.) Who remembers the story of when Jesus calms the storm? Does anyone remember how the Bible describes the disciples after Jesus calmed the storm? *And they* [the disciples] *were filled with great fear and said to one another, "Who then is this, that even the wind and the sea obey him?"* (Mark 4:41 ESV). In the story we just learned of the disobedience of Adam and Eve, is there any description of emotion mentioned?

Adam answered, "I was afraid because I was naked." God warns us not to subtract anything from His Word. I wonder; could we be guilty of doing this when we leave out emotions from our communication of Scripture when the Bible clearly states the emotion is there? [Pause for answer.] Interesting... are there any other emotions implied in the story? [Pause for answer.] How about the curiosity or desire of the woman for the fruit? Can we see from the story that this emotion is clearly evident? [Pause for answer.]

Here is the rule we need to remember when communicating God's Word. If an emotion or action is stated or clearly inferred, we need to include it. How do we determine if an emotion is clearly inferred? We need to ask, "Are there other reasonable emotions from the context of the story?" If it is obvious there is an emotion and there is nothing in the story that would contradict that emotion, then we need to represent it well. If there are other equal and possible emotions from the context of Scripture, and if the emotions are not clear, we do not want to embellish and we must handle those parts in a more neutral style. Remember, our aim is always accuracy in Scripture.

Now, let's test this concerning actions. The story says that after the woman realized the fruit would make her wise, "she took of the fruit." Now, what are all the possible ways she could have taken of the fruit? It does not say she reached out, but it makes the most sense and fits with the story. It is possible she went bobbing for apples and did not use her hands, but this is not likely, considering she then gave it to her husband. Also, consider how God made human bodies and observe that most fruit trees would require someone to reach through the branches to obtain the fruit. Not only does this make sense, but it does not distract. Therefore, when saying the woman "took of the fruit and ate and Eve also gave it to her husband, who was with her," it is appropriate to reach out for the fruit to show the gesture of eating the fruit and then handing the fruit to her husband. This does not add or subtract from the story, but accurately communicates the story in a way that is better remembered.

Now, we are going to form into groups of three or four and have each of you practice telling the story you just learned. Include the actions and expressions that are clearly communicated in the story. (Allow roughly 5 – 8 minutes for the small group practice.)

Choices

How often do we hear the phrase, "You cannot judge a book by its cover?" We need to read the book to observe the style and content. The Bible warns us not to have a judgmental spirit, but Scripture does encourage us to make good judgments. It also says, we will know if someone is a disciple of Christ, by his or her "fruit." A disciple desires to gain spiritual insight, wisdom and discernment of the absolute truth of God's Word, and with time, we can judge someone's fruit by the choices he or she makes.

Choices reveal people's character. As we teach Scripture, it is important that we convey the choices of Bible characters and the choices of God so that we can provide spiritual insight with examples. Proverbs 4:26 teaches us to *ponder the path of your feet; then all your ways will be sure* (ESV). The Bible uses the words "path" and "ways" as descriptions for choices.

What do we learn when we "ponder" our choices? In the Witness Development Evangelism process we use questions about choices to help people discover spiritual insight and to give room for the Holy Spirit to convict the hearts of people to reveal truth and/or sin.

Questions for Discovery

As we progress through teaching every story, a process of going through a five-part process using statements and questions will help us discover spiritual truths and insights and nurture a good conversation with others. These five are:

 Lead them through the story a section at a time.

 We point out the choices of what people and God/Jesus have said or done in each section.

 We ask, "What other choices could they have made?"

 By the choices they did make, what do we learn about that person spiritually or about their heart?

 Last of all, we state the result or impact of their choice to move them along to the next section of the story.

Parts and Purposes / Palm Pilot

Let's look at each of these in more detail as we look at the first part of Adam and Eve's story.

 Once you have told the story to someone, how many times have they heard it? *Once.* Everyone needs to hear a story at least twice to begin to remember the story accurately and then discover spiritual insights. In the lead through, we invite the listener to tell sections of the story with us. We simply retell a part of the story and then ask specific questions about what someone said or did. We do not include the introduction in the lead through; we start at the beginning of the story.

We start the lead through by inviting listeners to look closely at the story with us so that we can see what insights we discover. With the story of Adam and Eve, we ask several review questions. For example: The story from the Bible said, "So when the woman saw that the fruit was good for…" Do you remember what that was? (Food.) And it was pleasing to the…what? (Eyes.) It was desirable for obtaining…? (Wisdom.) What did she do? (She ate of the fruit.)

As I am leading you through this story, do you notice what actions I am doing? Our actions create visual cues. There are three interactive ways you can *lead* someone *through* a section of the story.

First, ask a specific question about an action or object. We want to avoid general questions like, "What happened next?" Our goal is for the person to be so successful in helping us in the story that they are impacted by the story and not stressed by trying to get the "right" answer. We do not want a teacher-student relationship in that they feel we are grilling them for the right answer. Instead, we adopt a fellow traveler attitude, wherein we humbly discover and share with them on the journey. The first specific question I asked in the lead through was, "When the woman saw that the fruit was good for something, do you remember what that was?" Note that as I ask this, I am holding my hand next to my mouth as if I was about to bite a piece of fruit.

The second option is fill in the blank. I used this when I asked about Eve desiring wisdom. "It was desirable for obtaining...?" Notice that I pause and wait for an answer while pointing to my temple.

Third option is to use humor or contrast to bring attention to and lighten the conversation. For example, after I said, "And she saw it was desirable for obtaining wisdom," I may give a rhetorical reply by saying, "But she knew better so she slapped the serpent, cut off its head and ate the meat. Right? No, she did not do that. What did she do?" Here I would pause for a response before saying, "Yes, that's right. She took of the fruit and ate it."

The only rule for humor is that we should only use it once, or we may confuse the listeners and distract them from the true story.

 Once we have led a person through a section of Scripture, we immediately point out the choices made in that section. We see that Eve listened to the advice of the serpent and then trusted her judgment that the fruit was good for food, pleasing to the eye, and useful for obtaining wisdom.

Here we ask about what other choices Eve could have made.

 Next, we explore what we learn about Eve from the choices she made.

 Finally, we look at the outcome of her choice. The result of Eve's [fill in the blank with their insights - disobedience, selfishness, etc.] is that she gave the fruit to whom? And where was Adam? (With her.)

Now, we are immediately into the next section of Scripture, and we can start the lead through with that portion of the story and we go through all five steps again.

The Palm Pilot

One way of remembering these five steps is by using your hand. I like to think of it as your "Palm Pilot." Open your hand with all five fingers spread out and you are looking at your Palm Pilot. The thumb points sideways to **lead** them **through** the story. The finger reminds us to **point out their choices.** The middle finger reminds us there are many choices on all sides so we ask them what **other choices** the person or God could have made. The ring finger is a memorial so we ask, "**What do we learn** about the person or God?" The pinky reminds us to **move to the result**.

One more time: the thumb is the lead through, the pointer is for pointing out the choices, the middle finger is for choices on all sides, so we ask what other choices could they have made.

The ring finger is to ask what we learn about the person or God and the pinky is to move to the next section of results. Take a minute to read your five-fingered Palm Pilot to the person next to you.

***

Let's go through the rest of the story using the five-fingered Palm Pilot approach. Turn to your practice buddy, or buddies, and each take a turn using your five-fingered Palm Pilot. You have several minutes to do this.

***

Application of the Bible Stories

By asking people questions, we help them enter and feel the story. We want them to experience the emotion of a story as if they were watching firsthand. As we help them discover spiritual insights into a story, they will naturally begin to apply it. We help in this process by asking application questions at the end of our presentation. For instance, we observed that the immediate result after Adam and Eve's disobedience of eating the fruit was they felt shame in seeing they were naked and they sewed fig leaves to cover themselves. At the end of the story, we see that God sacrifices an innocent animal and they are clothed with leather.

As we help people apply the concepts from this Scripture, we can ask, "Today, are you trying to cover your disobedience on your own, similar to what Adam and Eve did with fig leaves?

Have you experienced a time that God covered the shame of bad choices and sin with His sacrifice?"

Possible response if the person answers with fig leaves: By learning from God's story in the Bible, what needs to happen to you today in order to receive God's covering for your disobedience? How can I pray for you?

Possible response if the person answers with sacrifice of skins: Wow, great answer. If you are comfortable, I would love to hear your testimony of when you first experienced God's provision of covering your disobedience.

Now, let's practice this conversation with someone sitting next to you.

***

Context - Introducing Bible Stories

In preparing to tell a Bible story, setting the scene or context is important. Below are ways to decide what goes into an introduction to a story.

Context: To understand Bible stories correctly, many times the setting (what has happened before the story takes place) must be known. The essential information needed to help listeners best understand a story can be told before the story is shared. We especially look for spiritual context. What is God doing in the lives of the people in the story and how are they responding to God?

For instance, in the story of Adam and Eve's fall, it is critical that the listener understands that God commanded Adam not to eat of the Tree of Knowledge of Good and Evil and warned him of the consequences of death the day he ate of it. Adam was given authority over every living thing to rule on the earth and subdue it.

Terms explained: Terms that may not be understood by the listener need to be explained. For instance, words such as synagogue, altar, sons of the prophets, scribes, etc. may need explanation.

How and when to form an introduction: As you go through a story in preparation, you will notice what might be needed in an introduction. Just set that information on an imaginary shelf. When you know what you plan to bring up for discussion and what is needed for clarity that is not contained in the story, then pull off the shelf only the information that is needed to prepare your introduction.

Importance of context clarity: Sometimes, when you tell a story, you will encounter confusion on some issues. Only then do you realize it would have helped in the discussion if you had put a small piece of information into the introduction for clarity. So, next time you tell that story, you can add that information (as long as it is found in Scripture).

Let's form into groups of three or four and discuss the critical parts that need to be included in the Genesis 3, Disobedience of Adam and Eve Story.

Break

Let's take a break for [insert number] minutes. Please meet back in this room at [insert time]. We will start sharply at the end of the break, since we want to use every minute available. [Give instructions for where bathrooms are located, as well as snacks and drinks. Encourage others to take SOM newsletters and materials.]

PART IV

Witness Development Evangelism

Friday Night Workshop

Demonstrate the Disobedience
of Adam and Eve Story

Let's walk through an example of a conversation. (May I
have a volunteer?) Remember we use the Palm Pilot method
for each section and/or character in the Bible story. As we begin
the conversation, we want to disclose who we are, qualify our
reason for approaching them, and ask their name right away.
We also want to obtain permission to continue the discussion.
Your dialog might go something like this:

> **Team member**: Hi, would you like a gift? [Hand
> a tract.] I'm [*insert name*]. [Wait for them to state
> their name.] (Disclosure and qualify; use name
> immediately)
>
> [Insert their name], I am out here today simply
> to bless people in the name of Jesus and to see if
> you might allow me to pray for a specific need you
> have, or if you might allow me to share an encour-
> aging Bible story with you. (Permission)

Do you have a few minutes for me to share a Bible story I just learned, or maybe I can pray for you? Have you ever heard the story that explains where suffering and death originated?

First possible response: Yeah, I think so. Adam and Eve when they ate the apple?

Team member: Wow, I'm impressed. Many people have added and taken things away from this story over the years to fit their own ideas. Let me tell you how God described it right, from His Word.

Second possible response: No, I'm not exactly sure which story you're referring to.

Team member: Great, I'm really excited to share it with you.

Introduction-The Disobedience of Adam and Eve Story

Once you have permission to share, continue with an introduction to the Bible story:

In the Bible it says God created Man (Adam) and Woman (Eve) in His image and likeness. [We establish what God says in the Bible as we begin the conversation.] God blessed them and put them in a perfect garden with provision for everything they needed. He gave them permission to partake in all that He had given them. He put two special trees in the middle of the garden. One was the Tree of (eternal) Life, which they could eat from freely. The second was the Tree of Knowledge of Good and Evil.

God gave Adam a commandment and told him not to eat of the Tree of Knowledge of Good and Evil. He warned him saying, "The day you eat of this tree you will die."

God gave authority and dominion over the earth to Adam and Eve, even over the creatures that moved along the ground.

Next, the Bible says Satan came as a serpent and tried to entice Adam and Eve to question God and to break faith in His goodness and told Adam and Eve they would *not* die, but their eyes would be opened and they would be like God, knowing good and evil.

Tell the Story from the Word of God

[Tell story with animation]

> *So when the woman saw that the fruit was good for food, and that it was a delight to the eyes, and that the fruit was to be desired to make one wise, she took the fruit and ate, and she also gave some to her husband who was with her, and he ate. Then the eyes of both were opened, and they knew that they were naked. And Adam and Eve sewed fig leaves together and made themselves clothes. And Adam and Eve heard the sound of the LORD God walking in the garden in the cool of the day, and the man and his wife hid themselves from the presence of the LORD God among the trees of the garden. But the LORD God called to the man and said to him, "Where are you?" And he said, "I heard your voice in the garden, and I was afraid, because I was*

naked, and I hid myself." (Genesis 3:6-10 paraphrased from ESV)

This is where you end the story from the Word of God, but it is important to mention that at the end of this story God killed an animal so that He could provide them with coverings made of animal skins. He cut Adam and Eve off from the Tree of Life and He kicked them out of the garden for good.

Now that you have shared the first part of the story, lead the person through the story using the Palm Pilot approach to look at observations about Eve, Adam and God.

Palm Pilot: Observations about Eve

 Let's look at this story one more time and you can help me out.

Do you remember how the woman saw that the fruit was good for... what? (Food.)

And that it was a delight to... what? (To her eyes.)

And that the fruit was to be desired to make one... what? (Wise.)

Then what did she do? (She ate of the tree.)

 We see that Eve made the choice to disobey God's command when enticed by her greater desire for the food, the pleasure to her eyes, and her desire for wisdom.

What other choices could she have made?

 Since Eve did not do that, but chose to disobey God, what do we learn about Eve at this point in the story?

 Okay, now where was Adam during all this? (Next to her.)

Observations about Adam

 Eve gave the fruit to her husband, who was with her. And what did he do? (He ate it.)

 Adam also chose to disobey God.

 What are some other choices he could have made?

 Adam did not make any of those choices. By Adam's choice to remain passive and not do anything, what does this teach us about him? (Hopeful response: Adam relinquished his God-given authority and dominion to the serpent, let the serpent deceive his wife, and then partook in the rebellion. Adam failed.)

The result of this is that their eyes were opened and what did they see? (They were naked.)

How did they deal with their nakedness? (They made clothes to cover themselves out of fig leaves.)

Observations about God

 As we continue in the story, do you remember what Adam and Eve heard in the garden? (They heard the voice of God in the Garden.) Do you remember what they did next? (They hid themselves in the midst of the trees.)

And what question did God ask Adam? ("Adam where are you?")

 Did God really lose Adam? (No, but God chose to use questions.)

 What other things could God have said to Adam?

 Since God asked Adam this question, what do we learn about God? (Hopeful response: God holds Adam more culpable, responsible, and guilty than Eve. God loves Adam and gives him a chance to admit he was wrong.)

 Do you remember how Adam answered?

"I heard your voice in the garden and I was..." What kind of emotion did Adam say he felt? (Afraid.)

We were told earlier in the story that Adam was clothed with fig leaves.

Do you think the fig leaves worked to cover their "nakedness?"

Continue Discussion

After you talk through the Palm Pilot, continue the discussion with more questions related to the story of Adam and Eve.

Remember how God kicked Adam and Eve out of the garden at the end of the story?

How many times had Adam and Eve disobeyed? (One time.)

Do you remember what God said the consequences would be if they ate of the fruit? (Death.)

We see that God chose to sacrifice an animal in place of Adam and Eve for their disobedience.

What else could God have done? (Killed them, just kicked them out of the garden, etc.)

Did that animal disobey God? Since we see that God chose to sacrifice an *innocent* animal in place of Adam and Eve, what do we learn about God?

At this point you have two options:

1. Continue the Witness Development Evangelism method to the next part of the process, "The Good Person Test."

2. Go straight to God covering the sins of mankind through Jesus.

Today, are you trying to cover your disobedience from the ways of God with "fig leaves," your own solution, or have you experienced a time that God covered your bad choices with His "sacrifice of skins," his provision?

Possible response for answer of sacrifice of skins: If you are comfortable, I would love to hear your testimony of when you first experienced God's provision of covering your disobedience.

Possible response for answer of fig leaves: By learning from God's story in the Bible, what needs to happen to you today to receive God's covering for your disobedience? Can you think of an innocent sacrifice God has provided for all of mankind's disobedience today? (Jesus.) Have you experienced the covering of Jesus in your life? (If talking to an individual, you may ask, "How can I pray for you?")

Practice the Whole Process (Twice)

Turn to a partner and one of you practice and the other will play the person on the street. Go through the introduction, the Bible story, the Palm Pilot, and the discussion following.

Then, switch roles and have one practice and the other will pretend to be the person on the street.

***

On the Street Overview / Outreach Co-Leading

How many of you are enjoying this process of sharing the gospel? Have some of you gained new insights into Genesis 3? Would anyone like to share?

Do you think others would like to engage with you on this story also?

We are going to take the rest of the time to go out and practice what we have learned on the street. We want to divide you into small groups of twos or threes. All of you who feel like you have the basic process down raise your hand. Please go over to this side of the room with the instructors. [Pair those who are more confident with less confident participants. If there are enough instructors, make groups of three, pairing a leader with a confident participant and a less confident participant.]

Decide who is driving with whom and where each person is going. Are there any questions? You will want to try to be back at the church by [fill in the time]. We will not have time to share testimonies tonight, but tomorrow morning we will. You will want to get here about 15 minutes early to greet everyone, get coffee and settle in. We will begin at [fill in the time] sharp.

Here are some things to keep in mind: Just your willingness to go out and try is glorifying to the Lord. If you share this with Christians, how are they impacted? When you share this with non-Christians, how are they impacted?

How many of you remember the story of the sower and the seed? Who can name off the different types of soil? According to this story, only 1/4 of the seed bore good fruit. Expect at least three people to say "no" before you get one reception. If any of you are not able to share a story tonight with your group, then your assignment is to go home and share it with your family or call a friend.

Before you head out, let's talk a little about how the teams will work.

Outreach Co-leading

Oftentimes when we "street witness" we work in a team of 2-3 people. This is another place where you will see the value of co-leading. When your team engages a person or group on the street, typically one person will take the lead in the conversation. That is not to say that no else can talk, but at the point where you transition from casual conversation to spiritual matters, one person in the team will dominate the gospel presentation.

The rest of the team doesn't get to zone out. Others can comment appropriately, pray silently, or most importantly, deal with distractions. What is a distraction? A distraction is anything – a person, animal, or thing – that distracts your listener from hearing the gospel. Oftentimes it is a family member or friend. Another team member can engage the distraction and attempt to divert it from the rest of the team.

Members of a team should take turns presenting the gospel. As you practice co-leading, team members should switch roles between encounters. A brief and quiet conversation may occur to determine who will take the lead as you approach a person. One of you might say, "This one is yours."

Experienced team members should encourage other team members to take the lead during the gospel presentation. Thus, team members practice switching seamlessly between roles of trainer and witness.

Before you leave, let's pray.

Now go ahead and get together. I encourage you all to pray again in the car together with your small group.

On the Street Outreach

One hour on the street. (We will gather back together tomorrow.)

PART V

Witness Development Evangelism

Saturday Workshop

Testimonies from Friday Night

L ast night was an exciting time. We would like to hear a concise report from each group. Who would like to share? (Some questions to prompt more sharing if needed):

- How many of you were able to share a story last night?

- How many of you found it hard? How many of you found it easy?

- What was the hardest part and why?

- What was the easiest part and why?

- Would anyone else like to share a testimony?

Biblical History (HIS Story)

As we begin our second day of the Witness Development Evangelism Workshop, let's consider this question: Is the Bible mostly about us, or God? That's why we can call the Bible *HIS Story*.

God used mostly chronological order for the books and events of the Bible. In this, God shows us that chronology is important. He also urges us to remember His past faithfulness. The word "remember" in the Greek and Hebrew is used nearly 250 times.

How often did the prophets refer to God working in history when teaching? Can anyone remember the event most repeated in Scriptures? (Yes, the Passover and the Exodus.)

When the Holy Spirit came upon the disciples in Acts 2 and a crowd gathered outside the house in Jerusalem, Peter started with the prophet Joel and then quoted King David in preaching the gospel.

Does anyone remember the martyr Stephen's last sermon from Acts 7? He shared HIS Story, God's story, by proclaiming the gospel beginning with the testimony of Abraham and then working up to Jesus.

Who remembers the disciple Philip and what happened when he met the Ethiopian eunuch? The Ethiopian eunuch was reading from the prophetic chapter of Isaiah 53 about Jesus, who was like a sheep being led to the slaughter. *The eunuch asked Philip, "Tell me, please, who is the prophet talking about, himself or someone else?" Then Philip began with that very passage of Scripture and told him the good news about Jesus* (Act 8:34-35

NIV). Paul and all the writers of the New Testament continued to use HIS Story when sharing the good news. Who remembers the two men on the road to Emmaus? Did Jesus reveal Himself to them immediately, or did He lead them to the story of Himself using the context of the Old Testament?

How many of you like context? We ask context questions of each other. Where are you from? What school did you attend? What are some other context questions we use?

You will notice that every Bible story has context that helps us understand the story. When we tell Bible stories, we introduce the story first with the context.

Go - Proclaim - Everywhere

Does anyone remember the first commandment of God to man in the Bible? *So God created man in his own image, in the image of God he created him; male and female he created them. And God blessed them. And God said to them, "Be fruitful and multiply and fill the earth and subdue it"* (Genesis 1:27-28 ESV).

What is mankind supposed to make fruitful and multiply? What are we to fill the earth with and subdue it? His image. We are to multiply His image.

In Scripture we are repeatedly told that our purpose is to glorify the name of God. Glorifying His name can be translated into exalting, worshipping, elevating the name (or character) and reputation of God. Is there any other name that created mankind and can give salvation? No. Therefore, the hope of mankind is to make God famous everywhere. *In that day you will say: "Give praise to the LORD, proclaim his name; make known among the nations what he has done, and proclaim that his name is exalted. Sing to the LORD, for he has done glorious things; let this be known to all the world"* (Isaiah 12:4-5 NIV).

We notice a theme throughout Scripture of two actions commanded by God: Go, proclaim His glory. Who can think of biblical stories of God telling His people to go? Abraham? Moses? Elijah? Jonah?

How about in the New Testament? What about the Great Commission? *Therefore go and make disciples of all nations...* (Matthew 28:19 NIV). By the way, in both the Old and New Testaments the disciples of God were persecuted.

How is persecution connected to this command to "GO?" It was persecution that got many of the disciples GOing. Consider the stories in the Old Testament where Moses had to flee, David had to flee and Elijah had to flee. Now, consider what persecution did for the beginning of the church in Jerusalem. *And there arose on that day a great persecution against the church in Jerusalem, and they were all scattered throughout the regions of Judea and Samaria, except the apostles* (Act 8:1 ESV).

God used persecution to help Christians "go, proclaim everywhere." Can you think of some other stories where God has His people proclaim everywhere? (Examples: Joseph in Egypt, David against the Philistines and Goliath.) How about Naaman, the Syrian general, and the Hebrew servant? Let's turn this around. Does the New Testament have any stories that do not include some proclamation of the gospel? How about any stories that encourage a local proclamation only? Is this important to God?

Does God value and command humanitarian help in the Bible? In what ways does God command us to help other's physical needs? Examples: feed the hungry, take care of widows and orphans, visit those in prison, nurse the sick, etc. Why does God tell us to do those things? Because He does love us and wants others to know Him. As people know Him, they can glorify His Name.

The Bible says, *so whether you eat or drink or whatever you do, do it all for the glory of God* (1 Corinthians 10:31 ESV). Therefore, humanitarian help is good, but it is incomplete because God not only desires that we serve others, but also instructs us to verbally make Him famous.

Cat and Dog Theology

Cat and Dog Theology, written by Bob Sjogren and Gerald Robison, conveys the way cats and dogs view their masters differently. A dog says, "You pet me, you feed me, you shelter me, you love me, *you* must be God." A cat says, "You pet me, you feed me, you shelter me, you love me, *I* must be God." This difference between cats and dogs is very similar to how Christian theology is lived out today.

A person from the perspective of dog theology would say, "Lord, You love me. You bless me abundantly. You gave Your life for me. You must be God." The cat perspective is, "Lord, You love me. You bless me abundantly. You gave your life for me. I must be a god." Though they might never use these exact words, they make the gospel and God's glory about themselves.

People who come from either a dog or cat perspective may all look the same on the outside; they go to the same churches, sing the same songs, and quote from the same Bible translation. However, their frame of reference is very different. A dog hears John 3:16 with joy and says, "Amazing. Jesus died and now I get to live and worship God for eternity?" The cat hears John 3:16 with joy and says, "Wow, Jesus died so that I will not have to perish in hell for eternity!" The cat is not wrong; he is just incomplete – his focus is on himself. The dog sees the grander glory of living with God for eternity.

People from the perspective of dog theology witness their faith to others because they love God. They are delighted they are commanded by God to do so and they desire to give Him glory. People who come from the perspective of cat theology witness to others because God can save good people from hell and help them in life. As others are saved, their churches and ministries grow, which promotes more funds and activities.

Again, it is not that "dogs" are right and "cats" are wrong, but the motivations are different and "cats" are short-sighted. The reality is that we all operate with some combination of dog theology and cat theology. Certainly, this analogy can help us think of ways we can become more God-focused in our witness to a lost and dying world. We bring God more glory by witnessing to others about Him, and those who are saved increase God's glory and heaven's joy.

Turn to each other and share what motivates you to witness your faith to others. Share what prevents you from witnessing. In what ways are you a "dog" in your theology and in what ways are you a "cat?"

Witness Development Evangelism

Saturday Workshop

Witness Development Evangelism Process Demonstration

In the Friday evening session, we covered an example of how to tell a Bible story and followed up with discussion related to the Palm Pilot approach. Now, we will demonstrate the process with some additional techniques and stories. We will begin again with the story of the disobedience of Adam and Eve and progress from there. As we go through the discussion, keep an eye out for the parts of the process we have learned. Watch for things like actions and expressions, context to Bible stories, five-part Palm Pilot process, and application of Bible stories. [The Lead Instructor will demonstrate this with the whole group by asking the whole group the questions and allow them time to interact.]

***

Team member: Hi, would you like a gift? [Hand tract] I'm [insert your name] Wait for them to state their name. (Disclosure; use name immediately)

[Insert their name], we are part of a Christian dialogue team.

Sample Opening Statements:

- We are out today to build relationships and get to know people. Is there anything I can pray about for you? (Wait for response.) May I share a story with you that may apply to your life?

- We are out today meeting new people, do you mind if I share a story?

- We are out today to build relationships and talk with people about spiritual matters.

- We are out today to bless people in the name of Jesus by praying for any specific needs you might have or by sharing an encouraging Bible story.

(Obtain permission) Do you have a few minutes to hear a story? Have you ever heard the story that explains where suffering and death originated?

> **1st possible response:** "I think so. Adam and Eve when they ate the apple?"

> **Team member response:** "Wow, I'm impressed. Many people have added and taken things away from this story over the years to fit their own ideas. Let me tell you how God described it, right from His word."

2nd possible response: "No, I'm not exactly sure which story you're referring to."

Team member response: "That's completely alright, but I'm really excited to share it with you."

Introduction to the Story

The Bible says God created Man (Adam) and Woman (Eve) in His image and likeness. God blessed them and put them in a perfect garden with provision for everything they needed. He gave them permission to partake in all that He had given them. He put two special trees in the middle of the garden. One was the Tree of (eternal) Life that they could eat from freely. The second was the Tree of Knowledge of Good and Evil.

God gave Adam a commandment and told him not to eat of the Tree of Knowledge of Good and Evil. He warned him saying, "The day you eat of this tree you will die."

It's important to know that God gave all authority and dominion over the earth to Adam and Eve, even over the creatures that moved along the ground.

The Bible says Satan came as a serpent and tried to entice Eve to question God and to doubt His goodness. He told Eve she would *not* die, but her eyes would be opened and she would be like God, knowing good and evil.

Now, I would like to tell you that story from the Word of God.

The Disobedience of Adam and Eve Story

[Tell story with animation]

> So when the woman saw that the fruit was good
> for food, and that it was a delight to the eyes, and
> that the fruit was to be desired to make one wise,
> she took the fruit and ate, and she also gave some
> to her husband who was with her, and he ate. Then
> the eyes of both were opened, and they knew that
> they were naked. And Adam and Eve sewed fig
> leaves together and made themselves clothes. And
> Adam and Eve heard the sound of the LORD God
> walking in the garden in the cool of the day, and the
> man and his wife hid themselves from the presence
> of the LORD God among the trees of the garden.
> But the LORD God called to the man and said to
> him, "Where are you?" And he said, "I heard your
> voice in the garden, and I was afraid, because I was
> naked, and I hid myself."
> (Genesis 3:6-10 paraphrased from ESV)

This is where I stop telling the story from the Word of God,
but it is important to know that at the end of this story God
kills an animal so He can provide them with coverings made of
animal skins. He cuts them off from the Tree of Life and then
He kicks them out of the garden for good.

Let's discuss what we observe in that story from the Bible.

Observations about Eve

 Let's look at this story one more time and you can help me out.

Do you remember how the woman saw that the fruit was good for... what? (Food.)

And that it was a delight to... what? (To her eyes.)

And that the fruit was to be desired to make one... what? (Wise.)

Then what did she do? (She ate the fruit of the tree.)

 We see that Eve made the choice to disobey God's command when enticed by her greater desire for the food, the pleasure to her eye, and her desire for wisdom.

 What other choices could she have made?

 Since Eve did not do that, but chose to disobey God, what do we learn about Eve at this point in the story?

 Okay, now where was Adam during all this? (Next to her.)

Observations about Adam

 Eve gave the fruit to her husband, who was with her. And what did he do? (He ate it.)

 Adam also chose to disobey God.

 What are some other choices he could have made?

 He did not make any of those choices. By Adam's choice not to do anything, what does this teach us about him? (Hopeful response: Adam relinquished his God-given authority and dominion to the serpent, let the serpent deceive his wife, and then rebelled. Adam failed.)

 The result of this is that their eyes were opened and what did they see? (They were naked.)

How did they deal with their nakedness that they saw? (They made clothes out of fig leaves to cover themselves.)

Observations about God

 As we continue in the story, do you remember what Adam and Eve heard in the garden? (They heard the voice of God in the garden.)

Do you remember what they did next? (They hid themselves in the midst of the trees.)

And what question did God ask Adam? ("Adam where are you?")

 Did God really lose Adam? (No, but God chose to use a question.)

 What other things could God have said to Adam?

 Since God asked Adam this question, what do we learn about God? (Hopeful response: God holds Adam more culpable, responsible, and guilty than Eve. God loves Adam and gives him a chance to admit he was wrong.)

 Do you remember how Adam answered? What kind of emotion did Adam say he felt? I heard your voice in the garden and I was...what? (Afraid, because he was naked.)

But we are told earlier in the story that Adam was clothed with fig leaves. Do you think the fig leaves worked to cover their nakedness?

[Note the transitional question here, as the team leader continues the conversation] Remember how God kicked Adam and

Eve out of the garden at the end of the story? How many times had Adam and Eve disobeyed? (One time.)

Good Person Test

Do you consider yourself a good person? (90% of people will say, "Yes.") Have you ever heard of an ancient moral list of what is right and wrong? It is called the Ten Commandments.

Possible responses:

1. If they don't know, simply tell them that the Ten Commandments are God's standard of good and bad.

2. If they offer other than **anything** the Bible or the Ten Commandments, you may say, "That's good, but the one I'm thinking of is in the Bible."

3. If they offer the Ten Commandments, you may say, "I'm impressed; you're right. Let's look at a few of them. Which one are you familiar with?" [Use what they remember if they answer with any one of the laws.]

One of the Ten Commandments is: "Do not lie."

(Disclosure) Do you think I have ever lied? The reality is that I have lied in my life, many times. [If possible, give example.]

Have you ever lied?

What do we call people who lie? (A liar.) Now God sees everything and this is His law. So before God both of us are...? (Liars.)

Another commandment is: "Do not steal." Do you think I have ever stolen anything? Unfortunately, I have... [Tell your own story here, if appropriate.]

Have you ever stolen anything?

What do you call someone who steals? A thief. So before God both of us are what? (Thieves.)

Another commandment says you shall not murder another human being. Do you think I have ever murdered someone? (Let them answer.) Well, not according to the world's definition.

Have you heard of the person named Jesus Christ? God sent Him to this earth 2,000 years ago. Jesus spent a lot of time explaining the Ten Commandments. Jesus says that if you get angry or hate someone you have committed murder in your heart (Matthew 5:21-22).

So according to Jesus' standard I admit that I have had hatred in my heart toward another. Have you ever harbored hatred toward someone? So, in the sight of God, how does God see us? (Murderers.)

[Discussing the commandment about adultery is optional as the Holy Spirit leads you.] Another commandment says we are not to commit sexual immorality. Do you know what that means? (Any sexual activity outside marriage.) Jesus said, "Anyone who looks at a woman lustfully has already committed adultery with her in his heart" (Matthew 5:28 NIV). Have you ever watched a movie, read a book or even looked at a woman or man and had a sexual thought toward someone who is not your spouse? Therefore, before God, what are we? (Adulterers.)

We have just seen how we are already guilty of violating four commandments and there are six more we have not even touched. What do we call someone who breaks the law? (A criminal.) Would you agree that before God, we are criminals?

Have you ever heard the Greatest Commandment of the Bible? Jesus told us the summary of the law and the prophets. *"And you shall love the Lord your God with all your heart and with all your soul and with all your mind and with all your strength. The second is this: 'You shall love your neighbor as yourself.' There is no other commandment greater than these"* (Mark 12:30-31 ESV).

If you love an authority figure in your life, will you obey him? We have just proven that we have not loved God in our actions. Therefore, would you agree that since we have not kept the Greatest Commandment, we have committed the greatest criminal offense? (Have we loved God with our whole heart, soul, mind and strength?)

The Bible says that if we break just one commandment we have broken them all, because God loves His laws and keeps them (James 2:10). The Bible also says, *cursed is everyone who does not continue to do everything written in the Book of the Law* (Galatians 3:10b NIV). To be cursed by God is obviously very serious.

How would you define a curse? (Something that is bad.) If it's something bad, then what is the worst thing that God can do to a person? [If they say anything other than "hell," tell them that

Jesus said there was something worse. Often, people will say God could bring misery, sickness, or physical death. Tell them that Jesus taught all this and more.] In Luke 12:5, Jesus said that the worst thing God could do is to send a person to hell.

What is Hell?

How would you describe hell? Jesus taught three main characteristics:

1. Hell is extremely painful. He said there will be weeping and gnashing of teeth, burning fire and the feeling of worms eating your skin. (Not pleasant.)

2. Jesus said hell is complete darkness and bottomless (Matthew 8:12, 22:13). Some people have told me that they hope to be in hell with their friends. But even if their friends were close, they could not see them and they could not feel them because it is bottomless.

3. Last of all, hell is eternal (Matthew 25:41, 46). Even after 10 million years, there is no hope because you have not worked anything off. God is eternal, right? If we are made in His image, are we also eternal?

We have only two choices. One is to live with God, who is in heaven. The other is to live apart from God in that horrible place of torment, which is hell. Obviously, the seriousness of this is life or death eternally.

The Need of a Savior

What do you think we can do to avoid hell? (Common answer: "Be a good person?") Even if you lived a perfect life today until you died, would you make up for your past criminal acts? We still have a problem. What have we admitted about our past? Yes, we are criminals with a criminal record before God. This means, being good or obeying the Ten Commandments will not help. We are still going to hell because it takes only one violation to qualify us for hell.

Adam and Eve were kicked out of the garden for one act of disobedience. The Bible says we must be holy and perfect to enter into heaven.

Is there anything else you can think of to avoid hell? (Common answer: "Ask for forgiveness.")

Unfortunately, simply asking for forgiveness will not make us holy and perfect. Let me use an illustration to show why this doesn't work.

Drunken Driver Illustration

Suppose I am drunk and driving my car. I lose control, run off the road, hit a pedestrian and kill him. The police arrest me, put me in jail, and then I appear before the judge. He looks at the evidence against me and sentences me to prison. I say, "But your honor, I did not mean to do it and I promise I will never drive drunk again. It's my first violation and I have a family to support. Please forgive me and let me go."

Would the judge let me go? What would other people think

of him, if he did? Jesus said God is more just than any human judge. He is a holy and just God and therefore God will punish criminals. So you see, you cannot achieve forgiveness merely by asking. If God allows criminals to go free simply because they asked for forgiveness, He would not be just. Few people, if any, would respect God, and heaven certainly would not be a perfect place.

Let's consider other possible responses. Is there anything else we could do to avoid hell? (Another common answer: "I don't believe in hell!") What I have shared with you is not my opinion, but what the Bible says. My belief or your belief does not make something true or false. Truth is truth whether anyone believes it or not.

Truth changes us; we do not change truth. If I don't believe in gravity, does this mean I won't fall to the ground if I jump off a building? You will collide with the ground no matter what your belief system is. Jesus definitely believed in a real hell, and He taught a lot about it.

What are you going to do to stay out of hell? [Keep asking until they say, "I do not know." Then say, "You know what I found after reading the Bible? You and I can do...**nothing** to avoid hell."] [Pause.]

Was there anything Adam and Eve could do to make themselves perfect after they disobeyed? Remember how they tried to cover up their consequences by sewing fig leaves? Did that work? (No. Adam was still afraid and hid from God. But God went after Adam and Eve. He knew that there was nothing they could do.)

Do you remember what God said the consequences for Adam and Eve would be if they ate of the Tree of Knowledge of Good and Evil? (Death.)

Do you remember how God provided for Adam and Eve at the end of the story? (He gave them clothes from an animal.) So who died? (The animal.) Had the animal disobeyed God? (No.)

God took the offering of an innocent animal as a sacrifice for their criminal act. Wow, what other choices could God have made? What does this tell us about God?

The Word of God goes on to tell us that without the shedding of blood there is no forgiveness for breaking the law (Hebrews 9:22). Does this make sense to you?

This is the pattern God set up throughout history. I would like to tell you another story from the Bible.

The Abraham and Isaac Story

Have you heard of the prophet Abraham? Abraham was childless and God told him He would greatly multiply his descendants upon the earth and that many nations would be blessed by Abraham. Abraham waited a long time, and when he was an old man, Isaac was born. When Isaac grew to a young man, God tested Abraham and told him to sacrifice Isaac, his only son. Here is where we pick up the story from the Word of God.

[Tell story with animation]

> *Abraham built an altar and placed the wood on it.*
> *Next, he tied up Isaac and laid him on the wood.*

Abraham then took the knife and got ready to kill his son. But the LORD's angel shouted from heaven, "Abraham! Abraham!" "Here I am!" Abraham answered. "Don't hurt the boy or harm him in any way!" The angel said, "Now I know that you fear God, because you were willing to offer Isaac, your only son." Abraham looked up and saw a ram caught by its horns in the bushes. So he took the ram and sacrificed it in place of his son. Abraham named that place "The LORD Will Provide." (Genesis 22:9-14 paraphrased from ESV)

Observation of Abraham

Let's look at this story again and you help me out. When Abraham and Isaac reached the place that God had told him about, Abraham built... what? (An altar and placed wood on it.) Next, he tied up Isaac and laid him... where? (He laid Isaac on the wood. Abraham then took the knife and was about to do... what? (Slay his son.)

We see that Abraham obeyed God by building the altar, binding Isaac and being ready to finish the job.

What other choices could Abraham have made?

What do we learn about Abraham? (Hopeful response: He was obedient and trusted God's promise by faith.)

The result of Abraham's obedience is that the Angel of the Lord says, "Abraham. Abraham, do not... what? (Hurt the boy or harm Isaac in any way.) Now I know that you fear God, because you were willing to offer... whom? (Isaac your only son.) Abraham looked up and what did he see? (A ram caught by its horns in the bushes.) So what did Abraham do? (He took the ram and sacrificed it in place of Isaac.) Abraham named the mountain... what? (The Lord provides.)

Observation of God

God chose to provide a ram.

After Abraham obeyed, what other choices could God have made?

What do we learn about God regarding the need for a sacrifice? (Hopeful response: Even though Abraham obeyed, God still demanded a sacrifice in place of Isaac.)

Abraham was obedient and yet God still demanded a sacrifice. Why was this necessary? Abraham's act of obedience could not pay for his past disobedience. He needed a sinless sacrifice. It was God who provided the sacrifice. Who was the sacrifice for? (God.)

God provided a sacrifice for Abraham to sacrifice it back to God? And was that ram an innocent sacrifice? (Yes.)

Do you see a pattern happening here? Can you think of an innocent sacrifice that God has provided for the criminal acts of mankind today? Jesus never disobeyed and He gave his life as a sacrifice for our crimes. He was crucified on the cross and they put nails in His hands and feet.

As the nails went into him, what came out? (Blood.)

God counts the innocent blood of Jesus as a type of payment; it pays the penalty for our crimes.

Biblical Salvation: Repent and Believe

Since Jesus died for the crimes of humans, do you think we are all automatically forgiven? What must we do so that God will use Jesus' blood to take away His wrath on us for our crimes?

God requires that we do two things to apply this payment to ourselves: **repent** and **believe**, and we will be saved.

How would you define "repent?" (Common answer: Stop doing bad things.)

That is a *result* of repenting. In the Greek, repent literally means to change one's mind.

Do you remember when I asked you in the beginning if you were a good person, and you said "Yes?"

In light of God's laws and the fact that you admitted to being a liar, thief, and a murderer in God's sight, do you still think you're good? (Common response: Yeah, I think so.)

So, you think liars, thieves, and murderers are good people? (Hopeful response: No, I guess not.) [If they continue to justify themselves, then you can say, "Well, I'll continue to pray that God will show you the truth about this, but after hearing this today, when you stand before God you will have no excuse.]

[If they answer no, then you can say, "Thank you for your honesty. You have begun to repent and now you are half way to salvation in Christ Jesus.]

How would you define "believe?" (Common answer: To trust.)

The best definition I have found is to "depend upon."

Parachute illustration

Have you ever been skydiving, or wanted to try it? Do you believe parachutes exist and will work correctly? (Yes.) However, since you have never actually used one, then you have never had to fully depend upon it to save your life. In your mind you believe. You believe that when you jump out of the plane, the parachute will work correctly and bring you to a safe landing. When people jump out of a plane, what is it that they are dependent upon 100% to get them to the ground safely? (The parachute.)

You not only believe in your mind that the parachute will save you, you fully depend upon it to save your life.

The Word of God tells us that if we change our mind about our sin and depend upon the work and person of Jesus Christ, we will be saved from eternal death and hell and given eternal life and access to God (John 11:26).

The Three Crosses Story Introduction

When you think of the story of the crucifixion of Jesus Christ, how many crosses do you picture? (Three.) Do you remember who the two other crosses were for?

Jesus was crucified between two other crosses. Now, before I tell you this story right from the Word of God, I need to let you know that the Bible tells us that the crowd was mocking Jesus saying, "If you are a King, save yourself and we will believe." This included the Jewish rulers and the Roman rulers; even the criminals on the other two crosses joined in mocking Jesus. Here is where the story begins from the Word of God.

The Three Crosses Story

One of the thieves that hung on the cross next to Jesus verbally attacked Jesus. "Are you not a King? If you are, save yourself and save us!"

The other thief rebuked the man and said, "Do you not fear God? Seeing that we are condemned and about to die, we deserve what we have been given, but this man Jesus has done nothing wrong." Then the thief said, "Remember me when you come into your kingdom."

Jesus replied, "I promise that today you will be with me in paradise" (Luke 23:39-42 paraphrased).

Let's look at this story one more time. Please help me with the observations.

Observation of the First Thief

 One of the thieves that hung on the cross with Jesus did what? (Verbally attacked him.) The thief said, "Are you not a King? If you are, save…" whom? (Yourself and us.)

 We see the first thief chose to verbally attack Jesus, question his authority, and then ask for physical help.

 What other choices could the first thief had made?

 What does this teach us about the first thief? (Hopeful answer: "He wanted to save himself physically and tried to manipulate Jesus to help him. Not worried about death and judgment of God.")

 The result was that the second thief responded to him.

Observation of Second Thief

 How did the second thief respond? (He rebuked the first thief.) He said, "And don't you fear..." who? (God.)

Then he said, "Seeing that we are condemned and about to die, we deserve..." what? (We deserve the punishment we have been given.) "But this man Jesus has done..." what? (Nothing wrong.)

Then the thief said, "Remember me when you come into your ..." (Kingdom.)

 We observe that the second thief rebuked the first thief's mockery, he admitted his guilt, confessed that Jesus is innocent and that he is a king and then asked for help after death.

 What other choices could the second thief have made?

 From the choices he made, what does this tell us about him?

 The result of this man's choices is that Jesus responded to him and told him, "I promise that today you will be with me in paradise."

Observation of Jesus

 Jesus replied, I promise that today you will be with me… where? (In paradise.)

 Jesus chose to respond and promised paradise that day to the second thief.

 What other choices could Jesus have made?

 By Jesus responding and promising eternal life, what does this teach us about Jesus?

What was the main difference between the men on the other two crosses and how Jesus responded?

Remember how the Bible tells us that if we repent, change our mind, and believe, depending upon Him then we will be saved?

Did the second thief change his mind and depend upon Jesus? (Yes.) How?

 Where is that thief today? (Paradise.) Was he a good person? (No.) Was he religious and church going? (No.) What do you think of that idea?

Application of the Stories

Who do you relate to most in this story in your relationship with Jesus? Do you relate to the first thief or the second thief? Why?

In the story of Adam and Eve where are you today? Are you trying to cover up your crimes with fig leaves or have you experienced the covering of God through the sacrifice that He has provided?

In the story of Abraham and Isaac, we observed that God tested Abraham to see if he was depending upon anything else other than God. Is there anything in your life today other than God you are depending upon?

Like Abraham, have you experienced the provision of God for your crimes? How? How can I pray for you?

Why the Law?

Let's think back to where we started with Adam and Eve. Why do you think God gave the law to Adam? Does the law tell us what is good and what is evil? Does this meet the description of the Tree of Knowledge of Good and Evil? Before Adam and Eve disobeyed how many laws did they have? (One. Do not eat...)

The Tree of Knowledge of Good and Evil represents the law. Did God have to create the Tree of Knowledge of Good and Evil? Since He chose to create this tree, what do we learn about God? (God values free choice.)

By the way, since we observe that the Tree of Knowledge of

Good and Evil represents the law, what does the Tree of Life represent? (Grace and Jesus.) Jesus said, *"Whoever feeds on my flesh and drinks my blood has eternal life, and I will raise him up on the last day"* (John 6:54 ESV).

Does anyone remember ways that the Lord Jesus dealt with the law? Jesus said, *"Do not think that I have come to abolish the Law or the Prophets; I have not come to abolish them but to fulfill them"* (Matthew 5:17 ESV).

Jesus continued, *"Therefore anyone who sets aside one of the least of these commandments and teaches others accordingly will be called least in the kingdom of heaven, but whoever practices and teaches these commands will be called great in the kingdom of heaven"* (Matthew 5:19 NIV).

When the rich young ruler asked Jesus what he must do to have eternal life does anyone remember what Old Testament scripture Jesus quoted? Jesus quoted the law: *"You know the commandments: 'Do not murder, Do not commit adultery, Do not steal, Do not bear false witness, Do not defraud, Honor your father and mother.' And he said to him, 'Teacher, all these I have kept from my youth.' And Jesus, looking at him, loved him, and said to him, 'You lack one thing: go, sell all that you have and give to the poor, and you will have treasure in heaven; and come, follow me'"* (Mark 10:19-21 ESV).

Jesus ultimately used the commandment of idolatry to convict the rich young ruler. We see that Jesus had a pattern. He gave the law to the proud and grace to the humble.

The Apostle Paul put it this way: *So the law was our guardian until Christ came that we might be justified by faith* (Galatians

3:24 NIV). Therefore, the law has become our tutor to lead us to Christ, so that we may be justified through faith.

Teach - The Good Person Test

Right after we have told the "Disobedience of Adam and Eve Story," we ask the question, "How many times did Adam and Eve disobey God before they were kicked out of the garden?" (Once.) We immediately ask: Do you consider yourself a good person? (90% of people will say, "Yes.") Have you ever heard of a moral list of what is right and wrong? It is called the Ten Commandments.

Possible responses:

1. If they don't know, simply tell them that the Ten Commandments are God's standard of good and bad.

2. If they offer other than **anything** the Bible or the Ten Commandments, you may say, "That's good, but the one I'm thinking of is in the Bible."

3. If they offer the Ten Commandments, you may say, "I'm impressed; you're right. Let's look at a few of them. Which one are you familiar with?" [Use what they remember if they answer with any one of the laws.]

One of the Ten Commandments is: "Do not lie."

(Disclosure) Do you think I have ever lied? The reality is that I have lied in my life, many times. [If possible, give example.]

Have you ever lied?

What do we call people who lie? (A liar.) Now God sees everything and this is His law. So before God both of us are...? (Liars.)

Another commandment is: "Do not steal." Do you think I have ever stolen anything? Unfortunately, I have... [Tell your own story here, if appropriate.]

Have you ever stolen anything?

What do you call someone who steals? A thief. So before God both of us are what? (Thieves.)

Another commandment says you shall not murder another human being. Do you think I have ever murdered someone? (Let them answer.) Well, not according to the world's definition.

Have you heard of the person named Jesus Christ? God sent Him to this earth 2,000 years ago. Jesus spent a lot of time explaining the Ten Commandments. Jesus says that if you get angry or hate someone you have committed murder in your heart (Matthew 5:21-22).

So according to Jesus' standard I admit that I have had hatred in my heart toward another. Have you ever harbored hatred toward someone? So, in the sight of God, how does God see us? (Murderers.)

[Discussing the commandment about adultery is optional as the

Holy Spirit leads you.] Another commandment says we are not to commit sexual immorality. Do you know what that means? (Any sexual activity outside marriage.) Jesus said, *"Anyone who looks at a woman lustfully has already committed adultery with her in his heart"* (Matthew 5:28 NIV). Have you ever watched a movie, read a book or even looked at a woman or man and had a sexual thought toward someone who is not your spouse? Therefore, before God, what are we? (Adulterers.)

We have just seen how we are already guilty of violating four commandments and there are six more we have not even touched. What do we call someone who breaks the law? (A criminal.) Would you agree that before God, we are criminals?

Have you ever heard the Greatest Commandment of the Bible? Jesus told us the summary of the law and the prophets. *"And you shall love the Lord your God with all your heart and with all your soul and with all your mind and with all your strength. The second is this: 'You shall love your neighbor as yourself.' There is no other commandment greater than these"* (Mark 12:30-31 ESV).

If you love an authority figure in your life, will you obey him? We have just proven that we have not loved God in our actions. Therefore, would you agree that since we have not kept the Greatest Commandment, we have committed the greatest criminal offense? (Have we loved God with our whole heart, soul, mind and strength?)

[As the Holy Spirit leads, you can use honoring your Father and Mother or blasphemy of using God's name in vain. No more than four commandments are usually ever needed.]

We have just seen how we are already guilty of four commandments and there are six more we have not even touched. What do we call someone who breaks the law? (A criminal.) Would you agree that before God we are criminals?

Cursed by God

The Bible says that if we break just one commandment we have broken them all. Because God loves His laws and keeps them (James 2:10). Quoting the Old Testament in Deuteronomy 27:26, we read in the New Testament, "Cursed is everyone who does not continue to do everything written in the Book of the Law" (Galatians 3:10 NIV). To be cursed by God is obviously very serious.

How would you define a curse? (That's right, something bad.) In your opinion, what is the worst thing God could do to a human being because they have disobeyed His rules? [If they say anything other than "hell," tell them that Jesus said there was something worse. Often people will say God could bring misery, sickness or physical death. Tell them that Jesus taught all this and more.] Jesus said that the worst thing God could do is to send them to hell (Luke 12:5).

How would you describe hell? Jesus taught three main characteristics:

1. Hell is extremely painful. He said there will be weeping and gnashing of teeth, burning fire and the feeling of worms eating your skin. (Not pleasant.)

2. Jesus said hell is complete darkness and bottom- less (Matthew 8:12, 22:13). Some people have told

me that they hope to be in hell with their friends. But even if their friends were close, they could not see them and they could not feel them because it is bottomless.

3. Last of all, hell is eternal (Matthew 25:41, 46). Even after 10 million years there is no hope because you have not worked anything off.

I do not want to go to hell. What about you? What can you and I do to stay out of hell?

(**Common answers**) "Be a good person." "Go to church."

Even if you lived a perfect life today until you died, would you make up for your past criminal acts? We still have a problem. What have we admitted about our past? Yes, we are criminals with a criminal record before God. So being good or obeying the commandments will not help. We are still going to hell because it takes only one violation to qualify us for hell. Adam and Eve were kicked out for **one** act of disobedience.

Do you have any other ideas how to stay out of hell?

(**Common answer**) "Ask for forgiveness."

Just asking for forgiveness will not work and here is why. Suppose I am drunk and driving my car. I lose control, run off the road, hit a pedestrian and kill them. The police arrest me, put me in jail and then I come before the judge. He looks at the evidence against me and sentences me to prison. You say, "But your honor, I did not mean to do it and I promise I will never drive drunk again. It's my first violation and I have a family to support. Please forgive me and let me go." Would the judge let me go? What would other people think of him, if he did? Jesus said that God is more than just any human judge. He is a holy and just God and therefore God will punish criminals. So you see, you can't achieve forgiveness just by asking. If God lets criminals go simply because they asked for forgiveness, He would not be just, few if any would respect God, and heaven certainly would not be a perfect place.

So do you have any other ideas of how you and I can avoid going to hell for eternity?

(**Common answer**) "I don't believe in hell!"

What I have shared with you is not my opinion, but what the Bible says. My belief or your belief does not make something true or false. Truth is truth whether no one believes or everyone believes. Truth changes us; we do not change truth. If I don't believe in gravity, does this mean I won't fall to the ground if I jump off a building? You will collide with the ground no matter what your belief system is. Jesus definitely believed in a real hell, and He taught a lot about it.

So what are you going to do to stay out of hell? [Keep asking until they say, "I do not know." Then say, "May I share with you what I have found? There is **nothing** I can do on my own to avoid hell."] [Wait for this to sink in with silence.]

Witness Development Evangelism

Saturday Workshop

Learn and Practice - The Good Person Test

Now that we have seen a demonstration of the Witness Development Evangelism process, let's review what we learned, and practice it with each other. Let's review and practice the Good Person Test. Does anyone remember the two transitional questions to begin the Good Person Test? **"How many times did Adam and Eve disobey before they were kicked out of the garden?"** (Once) The second transitional question is, **"Do you consider yourself a good person?"**

We always assume that the people we talk to have little or no knowledge of the Bible. Therefore, in a non-condemning way we ask, "Have you ever heard of an ancient moral list of what is right and wrong? [Pause for response.]

If they don't know, simply tell them that the Ten Commandments are God's standard of good and bad. If they offer **anything** other than the Bible or the Ten Commandments, you can say, "That's good, but the one I'm thinking of is in the Bible."

If they offer the Ten Commandments, you may say, "I'm impressed, you're right. Let's look at a few of them. Which commandments are you familiar with?" [Use what they remember if they answer with any one of the laws.]

We do not go over all Ten Commandments. The reason we don't go over all the commandments is it takes too much time in most conversations. The Word of God is quick and cutting to the heart so one commandment is powerful in itself and we see this pattern in the Bible.

How many commandments do we use? The Bible mentions several times establishing two or three witnesses when dealing with matters. Therefore, we recommend using three commandments when sharing the Good Person Test.

We are using the Word of God to confront people in their sin. The Bible commands us to confront with gentleness (2 Timothy 2:25). Also, we are told to walk in humility. How do we gently and humbly present the laws?

First, we disclose our own failure: [Ask] "One of the commandments says we are not to lie. Do you think I have ever lied?" (Response: I am guilty; I have lied.) "Have you ever told a lie? When someone lies to us what do we call him or her? "(A liar.) "Since God hears and see everything, what would God call us? "(Liars.)

Another commandment says we should not steal. "Do you think I have ever stolen something, even something small like a piece of candy as a child?" [Give an example from your own life when you stole something.]

Take a moment to pray and ask the Lord what personal story you could share from the Ten Commandments to disclose your own failure. This would be a story you could share in conversation during the Good Person Test. [Give 20 seconds of silence]

After we have reviewed three commandments, we then point out that these commandments all relate to the Great Commandment. We ask, "Have you ever heard what the Greatest Commandment of the Bible is? "

Jesus told us that the summary of the law and the prophets is to love the Lord your God with our whole heart, soul, mind, and strength (Mark 12:30). If you love and respect an authority figure in your life, would you obey them? We have just proved that we have not loved God in our actions. Therefore, would you agree that since we have not kept the Greatest Commandment, we have committed the greatest criminal offense? We have not loved God with our whole heart, soul, mind and strength?

We make this point to help connect people to the fact that God is loving and holy. We also hope that people will see the depth of their sinfulness. We all have committed the greatest crime against God.

We transition with the Bible verse about being cursed by God: The Bible says that if we break just one commandment we have broken them all. God loves His laws and keeps them (James 2:10). The Bible says, *"Cursed is everyone who does not keep on doing everything written in the book of the law."* To be cursed by God is obviously very serious.

We have the person help us define "cursed" and then help them understand hell and the three important descriptions of hell.

Does anyone remember the three elements of hell we emphasize? (Pain, darkness and eternal.)

We end the Good Person Test with: "So what are you going to do to stay out of hell?" [Keep asking until they say, "I do not know".] "May I share with you what I have found? There is nothing I can do on my own to avoid hell." [Wait for this to sink in with silence.]

We wait for this because we want the Holy Spirit to do the work of conviction of sin. Without conviction, pride will make the mind and heart blind to the need of Christ.

Everyone, please stand up and make two lines of chairs facing each other. Sit on a chair and share the Good Person Test with the person in front of you. Then switch who shares.

Morning Break

Let's take a break for 15 minutes. Please meet back in this room at [insert time]. We will start sharply at the end of the break.

⁕

Learn - The Abraham and Isaac Story

1. Can anyone name one of the three ways we learn a story?

2. We listen to the story on an electronic device.

3. We listen to someone else read the story.

We read the story aloud and then we repeat as much as we remember of the whole story back without peeking.

What do we do when we listen to the story? We shut our eyes. We picture the story. We bring the story to life using actions and expressions.

This time we are going to learn the "Abraham and Isaac Story" and this time you may choose which way you want to learn the story. How many of you have a smart phone or audio Bible? How many of you want to try this way of learning the story?

How many of you want to listen to someone else read the story, raise your hand? [Divide them into pairs.]

How many of you want to read the story aloud by yourself? With all these stories being read aloud, this room will get noisy. Therefore, if you cannot hear yourself, speak louder. We want to give you an overseas cultural experience.

How many of you have participated in an overseas mission trip? How many of you have been in teaching sessions and classrooms that were noisy? You may have experienced background noises with the sounds of children, traffic, or merchants along the road. Most of the time in witnessing and discipleship opportunities, you will experience many distractions. All of us need to practice how to deal with distractions and work within these environments.

You may begin to learn "The Abraham and Isaac Story" in your preferred manner. You have 10 minutes.

Abraham built an altar and placed the wood on it.
Next, he tied up Isaac and laid him on the wood.
Abraham then took the knife and got ready to kill
his son. But the LORD's angel shouted from heaven,
"Abraham! Abraham!" "Here I am!" Abraham
answered. "Do not hurt the boy or harm him in
any way," the angel said. "Now I know that you
fear God, because you were willing to offer Isaac,
your only son." Abraham looked up and saw a ram
caught by its horns in the bushes. So he took the
ram and sacrificed it in place of his son. Abraham
named that place "The LORD will provide."
(Genesis 22:9-14 paraphrased from ESV)

***

Practice the Questions -
The Abraham and Isaac Story

Let's practice the questions and dialogue through the process of
this story. Who can tell me the five-finger Palm Pilot process?
(Lead through, point out choices, ask for other choices, what
do you learn, what are the results or impact of the choices.)

Who feels comfortable to demonstrate this process? [If no one
volunteers, have one of the Assistant Leaders demonstrate.]

[Have more volunteers demonstrate up front. If there are no more
volunteers, have them practice in small groups with each other.]

Practice the Introduction - The Abraham and Isaac Story

Can anyone remember what parts we put into an introduction of a story? (Spiritual context; in other words, what is God doing in the lives of the people and how are they responding to God? Explain terms.) What do you think is the most important spiritual context for a person to know about "The Abraham and Isaac Story?"

Here is what we recommend for introducing Abraham and Isaac:

> Abraham was a great prophet of God. He was childless and God told him He would greatly multiply his descendants upon the earth and many nations would be blessed by Abraham. Abraham waited very long upon God in faith and when Abraham was an old man, Isaac was born to him. When Isaac grew to a young man, God tested Abraham and told him to sacrifice Isaac, his only son. And here is where we pick up the story from the Word of God.

Practice the Application - The Abraham and Isaac Story

We hope that every interaction we have when witnessing our faith is to give an application to help people apply God's Word. This is not always possible, but we want to be ready for any opportunity. Also we realize that this side of heaven we are always limited by time. Sometimes our schedule is limited and sometimes it is the other person's schedule. We trust God's sovereignty in the time we are allowed to dialogue with others. Our goal is to be obedient to the Holy Spirit and to applying His wisdom.

In real life, we often only have time for one story or illustration. Therefore, we teach each part to stand on its own with discovery of spiritual insight and application. There might be instances where you skip ahead to the Good Person Test or the Drunk Driver Illustration...etc. We also teach how to bridge all the stories together as one seamless process. Let's look at the application of "The Abraham and Isaac Story" as it stands on its own.

We observed in the story how God tested Abraham to see if he loved God more than he loved Isaac. Today, do you see more people like Abraham who make God number one in their lives? How do their actions demonstrate this? Can you think of an example in your own life that demonstrates that your first priority is God or other things? Do want to share what that is?

We observed in the story how God provided the sacrifice of an innocent lamb in place of Isaac. We also observed that Abraham feared God, but still needed God to provide a sacrifice of an innocent animal. Today, has God provided an innocent sacrifice for the criminal acts of mankind? Have you experienced the provision of God for your crimes? Would you like to share how that happened? How can I pray for you?

We like to end the conversation with, "How can I pray for you?" Instead of telling them what they need prayer for, let's see what the Holy Spirit is convicting them of. If they ask us how they can be saved, we lead them in understanding salvation through the sacrifice of Jesus and what they must do to receive it. We do not want to lead people into a false security of salvation (Ephesians 2:8-9).

Keep these points in mind. We start by saying we observe, or we observed. This way every application is founded upon the story and not our opinion. We ask the application question with the word "today," followed by a yes or no question. Then immediately, we asked for an example of this application. Also, take a mental note that we start with the general audience of people to make the application non-threatening.

On the first application we asked, "Today, do you see more people like Abraham who make God number one in their lives?"

In the second application question we asked, "Today, has God provided an innocent sacrifice for the criminal acts of mankind?" Now that we have established a rapport, we let them give a personal example for personal examination.

We asked, "Have you experienced the provision of God for your crimes? Would you like to share how that happened?"

Would anyone in our group be brave enough to come up front and demonstrate what you remember?

Now we are going to practice the whole Abraham and Isaac witness process. One of you is going to share the story, go through the questions and then apply the story. I would like all of you to stand, please.

Practice The Abraham and Isaac Story with Mixer

In this next activity, you will begin to walk around the room. You will greet each person you pass and then move to the next. Stop when I say, "Stop, Proclaim!"

We will tell you which person tells "The Abraham and Isaac Story" process first. Go ahead and walk around the room greeting each other. [Let about 30 seconds go by.]

[Say, "Stop, Proclaim."] The person who is the shorter of the two of you will tell the first story.

Start with, "Hi would you like a gift? [Hand a tract.] I'm [insert your name]." [Wait for them to state their name.]

(Disclosure – use name immediately) We are a part of a Christian dialogue team.

Sample Opening Statements:

We are out today to build relationships and get to know people. Is there anything I can pray about for you? (Wait for response.) May I share a story with you that may apply to your life?

We are out today meeting new people, do you mind if I share a story?

We are out today to build relationships and talk with people about spiritual matters.

We are out today to bless people in the name of
Jesus by praying for any specific needs you might
have or by sharing an encouraging Bible story.

(Permission) Do you have a few minutes for me to ask you some
questions and tell you a Bible story?

Fearless Witnesses of Christ

How many of you remember where you were and what you
were doing when you heard the news of the terrorist attacks
on September 11, 2001? Does anyone want to share a short testimony? If we were old enough to be alive when it happened,
we have personal testimonies of 9/11. We can feel the emotion
and remember the details. It is our story and no one can argue
with it because we own it.

The Word of God says, *"And they have conquered him by the
blood of the Lamb and by the word of their testimony, for they
loved not their lives even unto death"* (Rev 12:11 ESV). Three
important elements here are:

- The blood sacrifice of Christ

- God's Logos Word

- Christ's testimony in us leads to courage

They did not love their lives even unto death. God offered His
blood for us. What does that teach us about God? How many
of you remember a moment when you felt God's saving hand?
Do you remember fear diminishing and being encouraged?

Does someone want to share? How many of you have felt the Holy Spirit speaking to you through His Word? How did it make you feel?

Jesus spoke of our testimony like this in the Scriptures, *"But you will receive power when the Holy Spirit has come upon you, and you will be my witnesses in Jerusalem, and in all Judea and Samaria, and to the end of the earth"* (Act 1:8 ESV). We are His witnesses. Witness in Greek is pronounced "martus" and is where we get our modern word "martyr." The word is translated as martyr or witness. Jesus gives us His Spirit of martyrdom and thus the name of our ministry. Our hope is that all believers would have a bold spirit of the witness of Jesus Christ and His Word in them. As witnesses, we do not live by fear, but by faith.

In the midst of persecution and threats by the religious leaders, the apostles Peter and John answered their threats with these words, *"Whether it is right in the sight of God to listen to you rather than to God, you must judge, for we cannot but speak of what we have seen and heard"* (Act 4:19-20 ESV).

One of the reasons we love witnessing the gospel of Jesus Christ to Muslims is that many people perceive a spiritual conversation with Muslims is dangerous. As we move by the power of the Holy Spirit, we experience courageous faith and grow deeper as obedient witnesses of Jesus.

Review Salvation

After "The Abraham and Isaac Story," how many stories have we told about God providing an animal sacrifice? (Two) Does anyone remember our transitional questions? Do you see a pattern regarding God providing an animal sacrifice? Can you think of an innocent sacrifice that God has provided for the criminal acts of mankind today? [We always affirm their interaction even if the answer is wrong. We kindly correct their answer, if wrong.]

We then describe the innocent sacrifice of Christ: Jesus never disobeyed and He gave his life as a sacrifice for our crimes. He was crucified on the cross and they put nails in His hands and feet. As the nails went into him what came out? (Blood.) God counts the innocent blood of Jesus as a type of payment; it pays the penalty for our crimes. Jesus is the sacrifice for mankind. He is even called the *Lamb of God* throughout Scripture.

Biblical Salvation

The Word of God tells us that Jesus died to pay for **all** the sins of the world and for everyone, but it is not automatic and not everyone will receive it. God requires that we must respond with saving faith. The Bible makes it clear that we must repent from faith in our own righteousness and believe in the righteousness of the Lord Jesus Christ and we will be saved.

How would you define "repent?" (Common answer: To stop doing bad things.)

That is a result of repenting. In the Greek, it literally means to *change one's mind*. Do you remember when I asked you in the beginning if you were a good person, and you said, "Yes?" In light of God's laws and the fact that you admitted to being a liar, thief, and a murderer in God's sight, do you still think you're good?

How would you define "believe?"(Common answer: To trust.)

The best definition I have found is *to depend upon*. Can anyone repeat the parachute illustration?

Parachute Illustration

Have you ever been skydiving, or wanted to try it? Do you believe parachutes exist and will work correctly? (Yes.) However, since you have never actually used one, then you have never had to fully depend upon it to save your life. So, in your mind you believe. You believe that when you jump out of the plane, the parachute will work correctly and bring you to a safe landing. When people jump out of a plane, what is it that they are dependent upon 100% to get them to the ground safely? (The parachute.)

You not only believe in your mind that the parachute will save you, you also fully depend upon it to save your life.

The Word of God tells us that if we change our mind about our sin and depend upon the work and person of Jesus Christ, we will be saved from eternal death and hell and given eternal life and access to God (John 11:26).

Learn - The Three Crosses Story

We want to continue to mix up the group as you work together. Think about how many letters are in your last name. Is your last name an even amount of letters or odd?

Please stand. If your last name has an even amount of letters, find a person that has an odd amount of letters. This is your new partner with whom to learn the story. [If more odd or even and not everyone is paired then have them use their first names or just assign the last few people with a partner.]

As a pair, you must decide what method you will use to learn the story or use a combination of methods to learn the story. You have ten minutes.

> Now one of the thieves that hung on a cross near Jesus verbally attacked Jesus. "Are you not a King? If you are, save yourself and save us!" Now the other thief rebuked the man and said, "Do you not fear God? Seeing that we are condemned and about to die, we deserve what we have been given but this man Jesus has done nothing wrong." Then the thief said, "Remember me when you come into your kingdom." Jesus replied, "I promise that today you will be with me in paradise." (Luke 23:39-42 paraphrased from ESV)

Practice the Questions - The Three Crosses Story

Apply the five-fingered Palm Pilot questions to "The Three Crosses Story." If you have problems, raise your hand and one of the instructors will come help you. You have 10 minutes.

Practice the Application -
The Three Crosses Story

After we tell the story and then lead someone through the questions, what comes next? (Application) Who can say the application questions for the "Three Crosses Story?"

Practice Introduction -
The Three Crosses Story

Now, discuss and form the introduction for "The Three Crosses Story." Think about someone who has never heard this story before and never read the Bible. What terms would they need to know and what context would they need to understand before telling the story? Take a couple of minutes to decide.

Practice - The Three Crosses Story Process

In your pairs, role-play with your partner as if meeting them on the street and share "The Three Crosses Story" process. You will give a short introduction of yourself, introduce the story, tell the story, use the Palm Pilot questions regarding the story and then apply the story. As soon as you are finished, your partner will take a turn.

Lunch Break

Let's take a lunch break for [insert number] minutes. Please meet back in this room at [insert time] (Approximately 40 minutes). Reminder: Encourage others to take SOM newsletters and materials.

Witness Development Evangelism Armor Illustration

Who can name all of the main parts of the Witness Development Evangelism process that we have learned? (Let the audience name a few.) We have created an illustration to help us remember all the parts of the Witness Development Evangelism process. We know that when we are evangelizing, we truly are at war and our battle is not against flesh and blood. We can divide the process into six main pieces of spiritual armor found in Ephesians 6:10-18. Imagine you are already clothed with the armor of God. Let's look at each piece from the bottom up.

1. **Feet** fitted for the readiness that comes from the gospel of peace.

   - The Disobedience of Adam and Eve Story (Genesis 3).

2. Stand firm, with the **belt of truth** buckled around your waist.

   - Good Person Test.

     * The Law/Ten Commandments.

     * The curse (Hell).

     * Drunk driver illustration.

3. Put on the **breastplate of righteousness**.

- The Abraham and Isaac Story: Declared righteous by faith.

4. Take hold of the **two-edged sword**, the Word of God which leads to conviction for repentance.

- Repent and change mind.

5. Take up the **shield of faith**, with which you can extinguish all the flaming arrows of the evil one.

- Belief: Dependence upon God (Parachute illustration).

6. Put on the **helmet of salvation**.

- The Three Crosses Story: Salvation message.

Connect Three Stories and Illustrations with Spiritual Armor

Please stand as we put on our armor. First, we think about the Genesis 3 story of the "Disobedience of Adam and Eve." If Adam and Eve had their feet fitted with the readiness to stand against the devil, they never would have disobeyed God. Let's fit our feet with the readiness of the truths found in the Genesis 3 story.

The second part of the Witness Development Evangelism process is the "Good Person Test." This is the belt of truth buckled around our waist. This is the truth that God is good and we are not. The law guides us to move from the curse to grace, or from death to life. Remember, the belt connects the top half of the armor to the bottom half; this will help us to remember to talk about the curse and God's judgment. Therefore, we need to wrap the truth of the Good Person Test around our waist.

The third part is "The Abraham and Isaac Story." God declared Abraham righteous through his faith. Therefore, put on the breastplate of His righteousness.

Fourth, we tell the illustration of changing one's mind (repentance). This can be illustrated by the double-edged sword of God's Word that brings conviction and leads to repentance.

Fifth, the parachute illustration reminds us to depend upon (believe upon) the righteousness of the Lord Jesus Christ. Remember to pick up your shield of faith that guards against the flaming arrows of the evil one and leads to dependence and belief upon Jesus Christ.

Last, we demonstrate salvation through "The Three Crosses Story." Christ is the head of the church and our way of salvation. He is on the cross with thieves, so let's put on the helmet of Salvation to remember the sixth part.

Now we are fully armored with the Witness Development Evangelism process and fit for battle.

Practice Transitions

Transitions help bridge the spiritual truths to one another. Like a string of beads, we want people to see how they connect. Transitions also help keep a conversation flowing and feeling natural. Let's look at our transitions from the beginning all the way through to the end. Who remembers some of the transitional statements we used between stories and illustrations? [Let the participants try to remember transitions and share them.]

Transition into the Disobedience of Adam and Eve Story

Let's start at the beginning. Who remembers what question we used to transition to "The Disobedience of Adam and Eve Story?" (Have you ever heard the ancient story that explains where suffering and death originated?)

After we point out that Adam and Eve were kicked out of the garden, what transitional question did we use? (How many times did Adam and Eve disobey God before they were kicked out of the garden?) After they answer, "once," then transition to, "Are you a good person?"

Does anyone remember the transition question after the law, "curse and hell illustration?" (Was there anything Adam and Eve could do to make themselves perfect after they disobeyed?) Remember how they tried to cover up their consequences by sewing fig leaves? Did that work?

Do you remember how God provided for Adam and Eve at the end of the story? (He gave them clothes from an animal.) So who died? (The animal.) Had the animal disobeyed God? (No.)

God took the offering of an innocent animal as a sacrifice for their criminal act? Wow, what other choices could God have made? What does this tell us about God?

Transition into the Abraham and Isaac Story

The Word of God tells us that without the shedding of blood there is no forgiveness for breaking the law (Hebrews 9:22). Does this make sense to you?

This is the pattern God set up throughout history. Let me tell you another Bible story. Next, we tell "The Abraham and Isaac Story."

After "The Abraham and Isaac Story," what transitional question leads us to the salvation illustration? (Do you see a pattern happening here? Can you think of an innocent sacrifice that God has provided for the criminal acts of mankind today?)

Transition to "The Three Crosses Story." When you think of the story of the crucifixion of Jesus Christ, how many crosses do you picture? (Three.)

After we are done sharing this story, we transition into how to apply this today in our lives. Don't worry if you forget these transitions. The process is not foundational. One of my friends has never mastered the transitions. He simply says at the end of each part, "Do you want to hear another story?" It is God's Word through the Holy Spirit that is doing the work in someone's heart and not the talent of the person delivering the message.

Tag-Team Witness Development Evangelism Practice

Please form groups of five. Each person in the group will take a part, and as a group, you all will go through the whole process.

The first person will introduce and tell "The Disobedience of Adam and Eve Story" (Genesis 3) and will share the transition. The second person will give the Good Person Test, illustrating the Law/Ten Commandments, the curse, and the drunk driver illustration. The third person will tell "The Abraham and Isaac Story" and transition. The fourth person shares the parachute illustration about repentance and belief. The fifth person will share "The Three Crosses Story" and the application.

The people in each part will role-play as if witnessing to four other people. All of you in the group will act as normal people. (This may be hard for some of you to be "normal," but try really hard.) Also, do keep in mind that this is practice; so do not make it hard on those who are sharing. We are also on a time constraint, so we do not have time to deal with objections and distractions.

This will take around 30 minutes, so go ahead and start with prayer and begin.

Divide into Outreach Teams

At this point, we need to divide you into teams of twos and threes. We want leaders and those who feel stronger with the Witness Development Evangelism process to go with those who do not feel as strong. Then, we need to decide where each team is going and in what cars. [Most of this should be done ahead of time with the host. Please plan outreach teams, places, cars and the time to be back ahead of time to avoid any confusion and to save time.]

The goal of this outreach is for each person to tell at least one story. If you can go through the whole process with someone, that's even better. Remember to pray together as a team. We will see you when you return at [give time].

On the Street Outreach

(Teams go out on the streets and practice what they learned.)

***

Testimonies and Debrief as a Group

Let's thank the Lord for all the seeds that have been planted and that all of you made it back safely. Some of you probably had very positive experiences and some of you more difficult.

Keep in mind that your obedience in witnessing your faith puts you in the elite status as believers, since the minority of Christians actually go out and engage directly in witnessing about their faith. Your obedience brings glory to God and the promise of reward from our Father in heaven. Let's celebrate this step of faith by sharing each other's experiences. We want each group to have an opportunity to share your experience and what you learned. Who would like to start?

Story Work at Home

Everyone has a homework assignment tonight. We are asking you to share at least one complete story with a family member or friend. If you feel led to share the whole process, you get double points.

Three reasons to do this:

1. This gives you one more opportunity to practice with someone who is not familiar with the process.

2. You will bless them with God's Word and witness the fruit of the power of the Word of God.

3. Sharing plants the seeds for you to begin to disciple, initiate and train others.

We are looking forward to more workshops in the future, that you will lead.

SOM Resources Available in the Back

As we have said in this workshop, you are a witness of the gospel of Jesus Christ. We are all called to make disciples. We consider you all partners in the kingdom work of Spirit of Martyrdom ministries. Our mission purpose is to glorify God by serving the church - the living martyrs - those who are sacrificing and risking much for the witness of Jesus Christ.

We hope that you might invite others to get involved with SOM. We have resources in the back, for any donation amount. Please feel free to give whatever God lays on your heart. If you do not have the money to give, please take the materials if you will read them and pass them along to others. These resources are far more valuable in your hands and hearts than going back in our boxes. Our request is that whatever you take, please commit to read and then give away to others.

One of our best tools is the SOM newsletter. Each issue focuses on a living martyr around the world who exemplifies faith over fear. Inside each newsletter is a prayer poster. May it be a reminder to pray for our brothers and sisters in Christ. If you know someone interested in receiving the newsletter, please offer to take their contact information and email it to the office, and we would be glad to send one. There is a basket on the table for any tax-deductible gifts. If you leave cash, let us know the amount by completing a "Witness Aware" reply card and list the amount for a tax-deductible receipt. You may also donate using our electronic check service or credit card by completing the information on the "Witness Aware" reply card and giving it to the Lead Instructor or by contacting the SOM office at 928.634.1419.

Are there any questions?

Ending Remarks on Saturday Evening

As you may know, SOM has an emphasis on witnessing to Muslims. Tomorrow we are going to give more information about how you can get involved globally with what God is doing around the world. We hope that you will begin to train and disciple others in this Witness Development Evangelism method.

SOM has two other workshops that help you go deeper. One is our Oral Inductive Bible Study Workshop. This workshop is foundational training in the discipleship of others by teaching how to study the Bible inductively in an oral method and then beginning to teach others. Last of all, we have our Muslim Outreach Workshop which disciples Christians in specific ways to reach out to Muslims. We hope you would be able to attend one of these workshops soon. When you complete an SOM workshop, we immediately consider you an Assistant Leader. Our hope is that you will help lead other workshops and build on your knowledge and skill. Once you show competence in a SOM workshop, we hope you will serve as a SOM Lead Workshop Instructor.

Tomorrow (Sunday morning), many of you will be going to your home churches. This is an opportunity to tell others about this workshop and invite them to observe tomorrow afternoon. Tomorrow will be a good picture for people to get a taste of the global work of SOM and the tools of the Witness Development Evangelism Workshop. Any questions?

[End in prayer.]

PART VII

Witness Development Evangelism

Sunday Workshop

Testimony Time

Who was able to share with a family member or friend last night? Who would like to give a testimony? [If time permits, add the following question.] Does anyone want to share how God has used this workshop in your life and what insights have you received?

Witness Development Evangelism Review

Let's take time to review together what we have learned. We always need the Holy Spirit to help so what is the first thing we always need to do? (Pray.)

Let's pray.

How many parts are in the Witness Development Evangelism process and what are those parts? (Five: the Disobedience of Adam and Eve Story, Good Person Test, the Abraham and

Isaac Story, Salvation through Jesus Christ, and the Three Crosses Story.)

How do we approach people on the street? (Up front about what we are doing to diagnose whether they have spiritual interest. We ask for permission to share.)

Who would like to share the introduction and story of "The Disobedience of Adam and Eve?" After we share a story, what do we immediately do next? (We use the five-fingered Palm Pilot questions: Lead through, point out choices, ask for other choices and what do we learn. Then, point out the result, which includes the application at the end.)

Who would like to take us through the questions of "The Disobedience of Adam and Eve Story?" What is the transition? (How many times did Adam and Eve disobey God before getting kicked out of the garden?) What comes next? (Good Person Test.)

Who would like to share the Good Person Test? (Use three commandments, the Greatest Commandment, define curse and define hell.) What is the transitional bridge? (When Adam and Eve tried to cover the consequences of their disobedience with fig leaves, did that work? Do you remember what God covered them with at the end of the story? Did that animal disobey God? So God used an innocent animal, as a sacrifice for their crime of disobedience?)

What story do we tell next? ("The Abraham and Isaac Story.") Who would like to tell the introduction and story? Who would like to lead us through the questions? Who remembers the transitional question after "The Abraham and Isaac Story?"

(Can you think of an innocent sacrifice God has offered us today for the disobedience of mankind?)

After the story, what illustration do we share? (Define "repentance," "believe" and how Jesus paid the price.) Who would like to share the illustration of salvation? (Parachute illustration.)

Who remembers the transition after the salvation illustration? (When you think of the crucifixion story, how many crosses do you picture?) Who would like to share the story of "The Three Crosses?" Who would like to lead us through the questions for "The Three Crosses?"

What part do we end with? (Application.) Who would like to lead us through the application? (Today, if you were to put yourself in this story as a picture of your relationship with God, which thief do you relate to more? The first thief or the second thief?)

When we think of Adam and Eve, do you see yourself trying to cover yourself with "fig leaves" or have you experienced the provision of God through an innocent sacrifice He has provided?

When we look at the "Abraham and Isaac Story," have you ever been tested? Were you obedient to God? Have you found God's provision of an innocent sacrifice for your crimes?

What is the very last thing we offer to people? (How can I pray for you?)

The Vision of Spirit of Martyrdom

As we have shared earlier, Spirit of Martyrdom's mission purpose is to glorify God by serving the church, the living martyrs - those who are sacrificing and risking much for the witness of Jesus Christ. Overseas, we serve the witnessing persecuted believers. Primarily, we build relationships with these believers. We serve them by coming alongside and discovering ways that we can equip and support their witness of Christ.

We supply Bibles, Christian materials and resources. We are training them with this Witness Development Evangelism process, the Oral Inductive Bible Study, house church planting, sewing schools and more. [Lead Instructor: Share a current SOM story to illustrate one of these works.]

Domestically, we are fulfilling our mission purpose by emboldening the witness of Jesus Christ through Christians here in the United States. We share overcoming stories in our newsletters and ministry updates of believers around the world in India, Latin America, various places in North Africa and the Muslim world. We also share regular updates on our Domestic Muslim Outreach and Witness Development Evangelism Workshops.

Domestically, there are three main components we are using to further the witness of Jesus Christ to the church in the USA.

1. We connect Christians to the global witness of the Body of Christ through our communication via electronic and mailed updates, speaking engagements, distribution of Christian books, DVDs, materials, and updates on current news through the website www.spiritofmartyrdom.com.

2. We have two components to help Christians grow in witnessing their faith and leading others in

discipleship. This training is through our Witness Development Evangelism Workshop. The other workshop is our Oral Inductive Bible Study Workshop. The Oral Inductive Bible Study Workshop developed out of a partnership with Simply the Story ministries. (This is another 14-hour weekend workshop.) We teach how to learn a story, how to ask questions and how to lead others. It is a comprehensive inductive Bible training and the foundation of the Witness Development Evangelism Workshop. We have introduced many concepts in this workshop, so you all have a jump start for the Oral Inductive Bible Study Workshop.

3. Another tool SOM offers to the church in America is our Witness Development Muslim Outreach. We train outreach teams called Christian Islamic Dialogue (CID) teams. These are Christians who go to mosques in America on Fridays to dialogue on matters of faith in Jesus Christ on the public sidewalks outside of the mosque. Our vision for this ministry is to equip Christians to adopt a mosque in America and to have regular outreach teams throughout our nation.

Why Does SOM Emphasize Outreach to Muslims?

There are 1.6 billion Muslims in the world. Do you think that God has a plan and a love for nearly 1/4 of the world's population? We are going to look at a biblical story of God's heart for Muslims. What worldview supports the number one persecutor of Christians? (The Islamic world.) How many countries are Islamic majority? (Forty-nine countries.) Every Muslim that turns to faith in Jesus Christ will stop persecuting Christians. Christians and ex-Muslims risk their lives every day to witness the gospel of Jesus Christ. If they can risk their lives in these restricted nations, certainly we can share in the United States.

An active witness of Jesus Christ is a tiny minority in the United States. We have a great opportunity to share the love of Jesus with Muslims in America. Muslims are coming to Christ; therefore, we have a unique time to lovingly share the heart of our heavenly Father to Muslims. In our experience, most Muslims are much more open to a dialogue on faith in Jesus than most other people in America.

The majority of Muslims in America have roots in restricted Islamic nations. If we can touch them for Christ, they can influence others overseas.

We have seen good fruit from a regular outreach to Muslims. Most Americans fear a spiritual dialogue with Muslims. However, as stated above, we have found that a vast proportion of Muslims were open to spiritual conversations. We hope you will ask God to give you a greater love for the thousands of Muslims living right in your local areas.

Next Step in Serving

It is our hope that all of you are energized by what you have learned and that two main fruits will come out of this workshop. One is a greater verbal witness of your faith in Jesus Christ. We ask you to pray for daily opportunities to share with others.

Second, we hope you will begin to teach others and help in scheduling and participating in other workshops. There are opportunities to serve here in the U.S. and overseas. As you stay connected to the ministry of Spirit of Martyrdom, we will advertise these opportunities to you.

Please pray about becoming a regular participant in our Muslim outreaches by joining our (CID) Christian Islamic Dialogue teams. For more information, please email us at: contact@spiritofmartyrdom.com. We also hope that as you stay connected to SOM, you will be inspired in your growth as a global Christian. There are many persecuted Christians who need our prayers, financial gifts, volunteer of time and advocacy overseas.

Why is Our Training Oral?

The uniqueness of the Witness Development Evangelism Workshop is that you have not used notes, books, projectors or any electronic tools. What has that felt like? How has this type of teaching helped you? There are a few reasons we have chosen this method. A practical reason is that if you have to write down you will probably not have the paper with you when you need to recall it anyway.

The most profound things in life are remembered. We are hiding God's Word in our heart pockets. We want this to become a lifestyle with memory muscle to support it. Do most people prefer to read a book or see a movie? We showed you that over 80% of people in the world cannot, or prefer not, to read or write. The oral method has the greatest potential audience of people. We want this method to be equally beneficial in the illiterate tribes of India and the highly literate areas of New

England. We hope that some of you are called to go around the world to teach this to others.

If we are serious about multiplication, then we need to exemplify everything we hope others will imitate. Most everyone can repeat oral teaching materials if given good training. But many people of the world cannot afford a computer and projector. Many do not have access to printers, books and materials. Also, in the process of translation oral translation is faster. Oral teaching breaks all educational and economic barriers. We have seen church planting movements around the world grow multiple times faster than in America, with less than half the resources.

Keep in mind that most believers in the history of Christianity never owned or read a Bible. The Bible says, "*faith comes from hearing and hearing through the Word of Christ*" (Romans 10:17).

We will give you a *Witness Development Evangelism Workbook* to review at home. Our hope is that you will review it and hide it in your heart so that you might freely give it away anytime and anywhere.

The Abraham and Ishmael Story

One story that is having a great impact for both Christians and Muslims alike is "The Abraham and Ishmael Story." We are also going to use this story to show you the power of Oral Inductive Bible Study. You will see many of the methods we have used in our Witness Development Evangelism process.

We believe this story is especially powerful for changing Christians' attitudes toward Muslims and seeing that God has a divine plan of grace. We also believe this story produces hope for all by observing the Father-heart of God for hurting people. Surprisingly, many of us can relate to parts of Ishmael's story.

During this section, the Lead Instructor will tell the story of Abraham and Ishmael in the full Oral Inductive Bible Study (OIBS) method. By telling in the OIBS style, the presenter should include all five steps of this method. This includes the animated telling of the story. Then, have the group turn to each other and repeat back as much as they can remember. Next, the "lead through," in which everyone participates and hears one more accurate presentation of the story. The fourth step is slowly going through the story and finding spiritual observations. The last step is applying the spiritual observations to personal application today. We encourage people to pick up David Witt's book on Abraham and Ishmael to glean deeper insight when preparing this story.

"The Abraham and Ishmael Story" is found in Genesis 16:1-13. Our time is limited, so we want to focus on Genesis 16:7-13 to see the relationship of God with Ishmael as his heavenly Father in contrast with Abraham as Ismael's earthly father. The presenter has the option to tell the whole story of verses 1-13 or introduce the story in verses 1-6 as an introduction to Genesis 16:7-13. The "lead through" includes verses 7-13 and the spiritual observations come from that section.

Introduction of The Abraham and Ishmael Story

For this story, we will want to remember that God spoke directly to Abraham and promised Abraham that He would make his name great and multiply his descendants. God would bless every family of the world through his lineage. God does not specifically name Sarah as the mother.

At this point in the story, God has enriched Abraham with hundreds of servants, camels, sheep and goods. Abraham's name has **not** been changed and he is referred to as Abram. Sarah is still named Sarai. Abram is 85 years old and Sarai is 75 years old. You also need to keep in mind that the area of Shur is in the direction of Egypt. There are approximately 200 miles of desert between where Abram is living and Shur.

The Abraham and Ishmael Story from the Word of God

Now Sarai, Abram's wife, had borne Abram no children. Sarai had a female Egyptian servant whose name was Hagar. And Sarai said to Abram, "Behold now, the LORD has prevented me from bearing children. Go in to my servant; it may be that I shall obtain children by her." And Abram listened to the voice of Sarai. So, after Abram had lived ten years in the land of Canaan, Sarai, took Hagar the Egyptian, her servant, and gave her to Abram as a wife. And he went in to Hagar, and Hagar conceived. And when Hagar saw that she had conceived, she looked with contempt on her mistress. And Sarai said to Abram, "May the wrong done to me be on you! I gave my servant to your embrace, and when Hagar saw that she had conceived, Hagar looked on me with contempt. May the LORD judge between you and me!" But Abram said to Sarai, "Behold, Hagar is in your power; do to Hagar as you please." Then Sarai dealt harshly with Hagar, and Hagar fled from Sarai. The

angel of the LORD found Hagar by a spring of water in the wilderness, the spring on the way to Shur. And he said, "Hagar, servant of Sarai, where have you come from and where are you going?" Hagar said, "I am fleeing from my mistress Sarai." The angel of the LORD said to Hagar, "Return to your mistress Sarai and submit to her." The angel of the LORD also said to Hagar, "I will surely multiply your offspring so that they cannot be numbered for multitude." And the angel of the LORD said to Hagar, "Behold, you are pregnant and shall bear a son. You shall call his name Ishmael, because the LORD has listened to your affliction. Ishmael shall be a wild donkey of a man, Ishmael's hand shall be against everyone and everyone's hand against Ishmael, and Ishmael shall dwell over against all his kinsmen." So Hagar called the name of the LORD who spoke to her, "You are a God of seeing," for she said, "Truly here I have seen God who looks after me."
(Gen 16:1-13 paraphrased from ESV)

Everyone turn to a partner, and the person with the shortest hair will repeat as much of the story as they remember. Go ahead and start with, *"Now Sarai, Abram's wife, had borne him no children. She had a female Egyptian servant whose name was Hagar..."* Keep on telling the story.

For retaining accuracy, let's go through the story one more time. "Now Sarai, Abram's wife, had borne Abram no... what? (Children.) Keep leading through all the verses of the story and letting the group fill in parts.

For time's sake, we are going to focus on the second half of this story and go through it slowly, looking for spiritual observations and insight. We learn from the story that Hagar became Abram's wife and then became pregnant with Abram's first child. When Sarai mistreated Hagar, she ran into the wilderness. At this point in the story, how do you think Hagar might have felt about her situation?

Do you think she felt protected and provided for by her husband Abram? The story tells us, *the angel of the LORD found Hagar by a spring of water in the wilderness, the spring on the way to Shur.* What clues do we have of Hagar's plan? What hope does a pregnant woman in the desert have of survival?

Next, the angel said, *"Hagar, servant of Sarai, where have you come from and where are you going?"* Hagar said, *"I am fleeing from my mistress Sarai."* The angel of the Lord just called her by name and noted her mistress, Sarai. Is the question, "Where have you come from and where are you going," for the angel or for Hagar? How would this question help Hagar?

Then the angel of the LORD said to Hagar, *"Return to your mistress Sarai and submit to her."* How did returning to Sarai help Hagar and Ishmael in their need? By the angel commanding Hagar to return, what role did he play?

Next, the angel of the LORD also said to Hagar, *"I will surely multiply your offspring so that they cannot be numbered for multitude."* Who was the angel speaking for when he said I? (God.) At first, whose plan was it for Abram to marry Hagar and have a child? (Sarai and Abram's.) Now we see that God had a plan to multiply the descendants of Hagar through Ishmael. What does this tell us about God and his relationship with Hagar and Ishmael?

Let's keep going. *And the angel of the LORD said to Hagar, "Behold, you are pregnant and shall bear a son. You shall call his name Ishmael, because the LORD has listened to your affliction."* What does the name Ishmael mean? (God hears.) Is this a good name or a bad name?

How many children does God name in the Bible? (You can name the blessed names on one hand. John the Baptist and Jesus are the two most famous.) Who usually names a child? (The parents or the father.) Abram is Ishmael's father and Ishmael is Abram's first son. When Ishmael was first endangered by the abuse of Sarai toward Hagar, what would you expect the father to have done?

When Hagar ran away to the desert alone and with Ishmael in her womb, who would you expect to have rescued her? What role did God take with Ishmael? What about Hagar? Would you say that God was being a good father to Ishmael? In what other ways have we seen God act as a Father? I wonder, was God having a vision and hope for Ishmael by multiplying his descendants?

God told Hagar, *"Ishmael shall be a wild donkey of a man, Ishmael's hand shall be against everyone and everyone's hand against Ishmael and Ishmael shall dwell over against all his kinsmen."* Interesting. What kind of issues and characteristics would you expect from a "wild donkey of a man who has enemies everywhere?" From this story, how can we describe the home in which Ishmael was going to grow up. What are the issues and difficulties that he must face? What would you expect the consequences to be of a young man growing up in this kind of environment?

We observe that God saw how Ishmael was going to be an angry, stubborn, independent, violent young man and we have observed God's fatherly interest and provision for Ishmael. What does this teach us about God?

The story ended with: *So Hagar called the name of the LORD who spoke to her, "You are a God of seeing,' for she said, 'Truly here I have seen God who looks after me."* By Hagar naming Ishmael, "the God of seeing" would it seem she was encouraged or discouraged by this encounter? What was "God seeing" that touched her heart and met her need? What do we learn about God and his plan for Ishmael?

It is worth mentioning that soon after this, God specifically said that he would bless Ishmael with 12 nations. What are some of the ways that God blesses his children?

We also learn that God commanded Abram to circumcise his family as an eternal covenant of God's plan and love for Abram and his descendants. Ishmael was the first mentioned from Abram's family to be circumcised. By the story, had God forgotten his covenant?

By tradition, Islam's prophet was in the lineage of Ishmael and therefore Muslims have inherited the spiritual lineage of Ishmael. Would anyone want to guess how many Muslim men are circumcised? Google claims 98% are circumcised while most Muslims claim 100%. Does this give us hope on God's plan and love for Muslims?

Two more details are worth mentioning in God's dealing with Ishmael. When Isaac was born and weaned, Sarah felt endangered by Ishmael and told Abraham to get rid of the boy and his mother. Hagar and 16-year-old Ishmael were sent out to the desert with only water and bread. They were about to die when God came to Hagar and said, "I have heard the cry of your son," and provided deliverance.

Finally, we are told in Scripture, "God was with Ishmael and he became a great archer." Now after going through this story, what new insights do you have on Ishmael and God?

We observed in the story how God saw the consequences of Ishmael's behavior as having issues with anger, abandonment and others. Today, do we see the consequences of this spiritual inheritance upon the Muslim world? What are some examples? Does anyone have a personal testimony?

In the Qur'an, out of the 99 listed names describing Allah, nowhere is the name of Allah ever connected with Father. Would you say Muslims today are looking for their heavenly Father's approval? We observed God's love and hope for Ishmael and his lineage. Today, can we find hope that God is working in the Muslim world? How do we see this happening?

Does anyone have a personal story? Now that we see God's heart and example of love, how can we apply this to our own lives and our behavior in dealing with Muslims?

We also observe in the story that much of the difficulties of Hagar and Ishmael were out of their control. Today, do we see people in difficulties and hurting from the results of other people's choices? What are some examples of a "wild donkey" and violent issues in the Muslim world today? In what ways can we all relate to Hagar and Ishmael?

Does anyone have a personal testimony of how they have seen this in their own lives or the lives of people they know? When we consider God's love for Hagar and fatherly love for Ishmael, how can this help us in the future?

[End in prayer.]

The details of this story come from Genesis chapters 16-22. I encourage all of you to review this section of Scripture and see what other insights you might gain and then share this story with others.

Final Witness Development Evangelism Opportunity

We want to take one more opportunity to witness our faith. We only have 45 minutes for this last opportunity. This time we are going to ask that you stay close and use the technology that you have for His glory. In a moment, we are going to pray and ask the Lord to reveal to you a friend or family member who would be blessed to hear a story.

Our hope is for you to call someone on the phone; you can even use Skype for someone overseas. We have Internet access, so any means of communication is fair game. If you cannot think of anyone, then you are free to go outside with a partner and pray for someone right in this area. For those of you who came to observe, we want you to shadow and listen to their conversation as you pray.

[Announce what time everyone is due back for the celebration meal and testimonies.]

***

Celebration Meal and Testimonies

Welcome back. This is our celebration meal of all that God has done over the weekend. He receives all glory; so let's first thank Him with prayer. [Pray.]

Once everyone is served we will begin to share testimonies and highlights throughout this weekend. Begin to think about what you might want to share. [Once everyone is served go ahead and start the sharing while everyone is eating.]

Workshop Evaluation and Resources

Please take a few minutes to complete the evaluation form and turn it in. We want to continue to make this Witness Development Evangelism Workshop better and would like to hear what portions of the Witness Development Evangelism Workshop were helpful to you. Also, remember to take any books and resources from the book table. These materials are for your encouragement and they are far more valuable in your hands as you share them with others, than going back in our boxes.

We will provide you with the *Witness Development Evangelism Workbook* for your review and further development. Please continue to pray how you might share this with others and please keep us informed of how God is using you to make Him famous around the world.

[End in Prayer]

Witness Development Evangelism Workshop Evaluation Form

We hope this workshop has equipped you with more tools to share the hope you have in Jesus Christ. We hope that you will begin to teach others and join us as Assistant Instructors for future workshops. Please take a moment to give us feedback as we improve our communication of His Word.

With one being low and five being high, please rate the workshop:

1. Before the workshop began, how would you rate your competency of witnessing your faith to others? (1 is little confidence and understanding and 5 is absolute confidence and understanding in sharing the gospel.)

2. After the workshop, how do you now rate yourself?

3. What part of the workshop did you enjoy the most and why?

4. What part of the workshop did you least enjoy and why?

5. What improvements do you suggest we make for future workshops?

6. How do you hope to be involved in SOM Witness Development Workshops in the future?

7. Are there other ways that Spirit of Martyrdom ministries can serve you?

8. Spirit of Martyrdom has the following monthly email updates. Please circle which updates you are interested in receiving. (Please add contact information below for SOM to update our records.)

   - SOM India Update
   - SOM Latin America Update
   - SOM Muslim World Update
   - SOM Domestic Muslim Outreach (Christian Islamic Dialogue Team Updates)
   - SOM Witness Development Evangelism & Discipleship

9. Please share any other comments, ideas or questions below.

"...You will receive power when the Holy Spirit has come upon you, and you will be my witnesses in Jerusalem, and in all Judea and Samaria, and to the end of the earth" (Acts 1:8).

Name: _____

Phone/Cell Phone: _____

Mailing Address: _____

Email Address: _____

Please give this completed evaluation to the Lead Instructor or email it to contact@SpiritofMartyrdom.com. Thank you!

Assistant Instructor's Questionnaire Form

Thank you for your willingness to take a step of faith and serve the Body of Christ as an Assistant Instructor for the Spirit of Martyrdom Witness Development Evangelism Workshop. Please complete this questionnaire and email or mail it back to your Lead Instructor. The Lead Instructor will assign you sections to learn and teach during our workshop. This questionnaire gives the Lead Instructor some insight into your skill set of teaching and learning style and helps them determine the best fit in assigning sections. Please complete as much of this form as possible.

Name: _____

Mailing address: _____

Contact phone: _____

Email address: _____

Skype ID: _____

Church or organization that you are affiliated with:

_____

Place and date of your workshop:

_____

How long have you been a Christian and walking in Lordship with Jesus Christ?

_____

Have you ever been trained in any orality method of the Oral Inductive Bible training or story-telling method? If yes, please give us details.

_____

What leadership and ministries have you served with in your church or a parachurch organization?

_____

Have you taught Bible studies before or taught Scripture in front of a group of people before? Please explain.

_____

Have you been trained in any evangelism method? If yes, please explain and how often do you find yourself able to share the gospel with others?

_____

Are you fluent in any other languages?

_____

Please answer these questions as 1 being low or do not agree and 5 being high or strongly agree.

_____ I like speaking in front of people.

_____ I would rather watch a movie than read a book.

_____ I learn better when I am moving around.

_____ I feel very nervous when I have to speak in front of people.

_____ People tell me that I am a natural leader.

_____ I have a strong desire to witness Christ to others.

_____ I can read something once and retain much of the information.

_____ I love to read books.

_____ I am afraid of trying new things.

_____ I enjoy theater and have acted in plays over my lifetime.

_____ People tell me I have a loud voice and I am easy to understand.

_____ I enjoy leading discussions when teaching a topic.

_____ I am more comfortable following others than leading a group.

Thank you again for emailing or mailing the completed form to your Lead Instructor or to the SOM office at contact@ SpiritofMartyrdom.com. We look forward to serving together with you.

Schedule with Sections and Time

Page #	Description	Time in Min.	Real Time (Fill in Time)	Instructor	✓
	FRIDAY NIGHT WORKSHOP				
2	Responsibilities of the host church or organization				
11	Introduction: Names of Leadership, Thank Host, Introduction to SOM Ministries and Purpose, Schedule Overview	5		Lead Instructor	
12	Unique Teaching Style	4			
14	Personal Stories	7			
15	Listening and Responding	4			
16	God's Example of Using Questions	2			
16	God's Example of Listening and Responding	2			
17	Stories Communicate Truth	2			
18	World Literacy	12			
21	Jesus' Model	4			
23	Learn the First Story – "Disobedience of Adam and Eve" (Genesis 3)	15		Lead Instructor	
25	Accuracy, Actions and Expressions	16			
28	Choices	2			
29	Questions for Discovery	1			
30	Parts and Purposes / Palm Pilot	10		Lead Instructor	
33	Application of the Bible Stories	2			

	FRIDAY NIGHT WORKSHOP (Continued)				
34	Context – Introducing Bible Stories	6			
36	Break	15		Lead Instructor	
37	Demonstrate "The Disobedience of Adam and Eve Story"	13		Lead Instructor	
44	Practice the Whole Process #1	13		Lead Instructor	
44	Practice the Whole Process #2	13		Lead Instructor	
45	On the Street Overview / Outreach Co-Leading	10		Lead Instructor	
47	On the Street Outreach	60			

	SATURDAY WORKSHOP				
49	Testimonies from Friday Night	20			
50	Biblical History (HIS Story)	3			
51	Go – Proclaim – Everywhere	6			
53	Cat and Dog Theology	4			
55	Witness Development Evangelism Process Demonstration	40		Lead Instructor	
77	Why the Law?	5			
79	Teach – The Good Person Test	6			
82	Cursed by God	8			
85	Learn and Practice – The Good Person Test	20		Lead Instructor	
88	Morning Break	15		Lead Instructor	
88	Learn – "The Abraham and Isaac Story"	15			
90	Practice the Questions – "The Abraham and Isaac Story"	12			
91	Practice the Introduction – "The Abraham and Isaac Story"	2			
91	Practice the Application – "The Abraham and Isaac Story"	10		Lead Instructor	
94	Practice "The Abraham and Isaac Story" with Mixer	12		Lead Instructor	
95	Fearless Witnesses of Christ	6			
96	Review Salvation	6			
98	Learn – "The Three Crosses Story"	12			
99	Practice the Questions – "The Three Crosses Story"	12			
100	Practice the Application – "The Three Crosses Story"	12			
100	Practice the Introduction – "The Three Crosses Story"	2			
100	Practice – "The Three Crosses Story" Process	14		Lead Instructor	

	SATURDAY WORKSHOP (Continued)				
100	Lunch Break	98		Lead Instructor	
101	Witness Development Evangelism – Armor Illustration	4			
103	Practice Transitions	4			
105	Tag-Team Witness Development Evangelism Practice	35		Lead Instructor	
106	Divide Into Outreach Teams	5		Lead Instructor	
107	On the Street Outreach	92			
107	Testimonies and Debrief as a Group	30		Lead Instructor	
107	Story Work at Home	2		Lead Instructor	
108	SOM Resources Available in the Back	3		Lead Instructor	
109	Ending Remarks on Saturday Evening	5		Lead Instructor	

	SUNDAY WORKSHOP				
111	Testimony Time	20		Lead Instructor	
111	Witness Development Evangelism Review	40		Lead Instructor	
113	The Vision of Spirit of Martyrdom	5			
115	Why does SOM Emphasize Outreach to Muslims?	4			
116	Next Step in Serving	2			
117	Why is Our Training Oral?	5			
118	"The Abraham and Ishmael Story"	45		Lead Instructor	
126	Final Witness Development Evangelism Opportunity	60			
127	Celebration Meal and Testimonies	60		Lead Instructor	
127	Evaluation and Resources	10		Lead Instructor	

For a printable, PDF version of this schedule, visit:

http://www.spiritofmartyrdom.com/witness-development

About the Authors

Pastor David Witt, along with his wife Cindy, is the founder of Spirit of Martyrdom ministries. He has spoken for more than 2,500 churches and Christian ministries in the United States. He has traveled to more than 50 nations in his lifetime. David has preached in underground church meetings and has met with house church leaders around the world. His heart has been touched and his life changed by their love for others and forgiveness for their enemies, even when facing death. Pastor Witt desires to share their stories and see the global Church emboldened in the witness of their faith in Jesus Christ and His Word.

Cindy Witt enjoys working in the Ministry Relations department for Spirit of Martyrdom ministries. She expresses what a privilege it is to work alongside our brothers and sisters around the world who courageously share the hope in Jesus Christ at a great cost and sacrifice. She is honored to work with the Spirit of Martyrdom USA office staff and dedicated volunteers who faithfully work together as a team for our brothers and sisters globally.

R on Kaufmann is the Director of Witness and Evangelism Development for Spirit of Martyrdom. He has traveled to Algeria, India, Senegal and Tunisia. He is married to Nadia, a beautiful Muslim background believer who is a partner with him in sharing the Good News of Jesus Christ. He oversees global biblical training and leads the Witness Development Workshops domestically and overseas.

Connect with Spirit of Martyrdom

Website

www.spiritofmartyrdom.com

Receive newsletter updates

www.spiritofmartyrdom.com/newsletter-sign-up

Buy books

www.spiritofmartyrdom.com/store

FEARLESS
In the Midst of Terror
Love

Rediscovering Jesus' Spirit of Martyrdom
With Meditations of Christ and His Love

David Witt
Mujahid El Masih

The Biblical teaching of Christian martyrdom is a call to intentional, purposeful living and a bold witness of faith. These fifty true stories of courageous Christians will bring encouragement, inspiration, and hope in the coming days of terrorism in America.

This book has teaching and stories regarding Biblical martyrdom, Islamic martyrdom and Christian persecution. But do not be intimidated. These are powerful subjects and they are written with the intent to bless you and change your life forever. It is first written for Christians who are looking for purpose and hope in these days of worldwide terrorism and second for Muslims seeking the heart of God in true worship. Our hope is that the fruit of this book will produce a fearless love to help you enjoy the journey of an obedient life that God intends for all His children.

You'll learn:

- About basic Muslim beliefs.
- How to reach out to Muslims.
- How to share the gospel with Muslims.
- How God gives faith that overcomes the fear of suffering and death.
- How a close relationship with Jesus Christ gives us fearless love.
- How to battle the global war on terror from the spiritual battlefield.

Available where books are sold

jubilee
B I B L E 2000

Hear what God is saying through this original translation

ANEKO Press